FRESH SPRINGS
ESSAYS BY TOM WELLS

FRESH SPRINGS

ESSAYS BY **TOM WELLS**

www.joshuapress.com

p r e s s

Joshua Press Inc., Dundas, Ontario, Canada
www.joshuapress.com

Editorial director: Michael A.G. Haykin
Creative/production manager: Janice Van Eck
© Cover & book design by Janice Van Eck

Note: Bible references throughout this book are from various versions and editions of the
Bible without specification.
Our special thanks to *Reformation & Revival Journal* for permission to reprint essays by
Tom Wells which first appeared on its pages. You can find out more about this ministry by
going to www.randr.org or by writing Reformation and Revival Ministries, P.O. Box 88216,
Carol Stream, IL USA 60188-9244

National Library of Canada Cataloguing in Publication Data

Wells, Tom, 1933–
    Fresh springs: essays / by Tom Wells

Includes index.
ISBN 1-894400-14-3

1. Christianity. I. Title

BV4510.3.W44 2002   230   C2002-903157-5

To Dr. Newton L. Bush, acquaintance of forty years, co-pastor with me at The King's Chapel for eighteen years, constant mentor and example, and beloved friend forever

OTHER TITLES BY TOM WELLS

Life of Christ
Faith: the gift of God
A vision for missions
Come to me
Christian: take heart
A price for a people
God is King
Come home forever
New covenant theology (with Fred Zaspel)

CONTENTS

FOREWORD

I have long admired Tom Wells' literary gift for exploring central and, in some cases, extremely difficult theological issues. He can cut to the heart of a matter, but never in a way that causes needless offense. Always firmly rooted in the Scripture that he loves, he is not afraid to think through a matter where others might fear to tread.

All but two of the essays in this collection were originally published in the *Reformation & Revival Journal*. They thus reflect, in part, the key emphases of that journal. Since 1992 *Reformation & Revival Journal* has appeared as a quarterly, seeking to encourage theological reflection on classic Christian orthodoxy, especially as it has been developed in the Reformed tradition. As the title of the journal indicates, it has two central goals: ongoing reformation in accord with the watch-cry of the sixteenth century—*ecclesia semper reformanda*, "the church always reforming"—and spiritual revitalization and renewal. Since the journal unashamedly glories in the Scriptures as God's perfect revelation, both of these goals are pursued in its pages with reverent submission to the Bible.

Tom Wells' essays well reflect these two central aims of *Reformation & Revival Journal*, encouraging reformation of our theology and pressing home the ongoing need to have a vital, living Christianity. All of this is done in joyful submission to the authority of Holy Scripture. It is a privilege and pleasure to introduce them now to a wider audience.

Michael A.G. Haykin
Dundas, Ontario
June 2002

PREFACE

The body of a book is difficult to write, a preface harder still. You want to commend your book to the reader, but the pitfalls are enormous. You run the risk of making the reader a gentle cynic that sees a young father showing off pictures of his latest offspring. Innocent fun? Of course. Reason to buy the book? Hardly. What then should interest you in this small volume? Two things, I think.

First, *Fresh springs* is biblically based, not in some vague general sense like one of those topical sermons that takes a text and then meanders away from it. Any meandering away from Scripture here not only is unintended but no doubt has already been ruthlessly pruned from its pages by my editors. That still leaves you to decide for yourself whether what stands here is biblically faithful. At that point it is you the reader who must be ruthless. I feel confident that you will agree that it is the Bible that forms the bond between you as reader and me as writer.

Second, *Fresh springs* applies to you, to your own pilgrimage through life, if you are a believer in Jesus Christ. Since I wrote most of these chapters some time ago, I was pleasantly surprised in re-reading them to find how applicable they are to where we find ourselves at the beginning of the twenty-first century. I guess it is not hard to explain that fact. God has not changed (despite the latest theological fads), and human beings face the same questions and difficulties that we have always faced. Were it not for the fact that we stand on the shoulders of the ministers, theologians, and writers who have gone before us, there would be little reason to go over these controversial truths again. But that is where we stand, so, with the Lord's help, we have a clearer view of the good land before us.

Of course you will make your own judgments about what is written in these pages, but I hope you will make the journey with me. And may the Lord bless you in doing it!

One more word. I am exceedingly grateful to John Armstrong and Martin Holdt for reading the manuscript, and to Michael Haykin and Janice Van Eck of Joshua Press for their friendly guidance and first-class editorial work.

Tom Wells
West Chester, Ohio
June 2002

SECTION I

Doctrine

1

WHAT DO WE MEAN
BY "THE WORD OF GOD"?

The question at the head of this chapter may seem a little basic for some readers, but it is of such central importance that we need to be clear about it before tackling other issues. There are a number of things that can be called "the Word of God," so let us see if we can sort them out.

First, I will simply note in passing that God the Son is called in Scripture, "the Word" and "the Word of God" (John 1:1,14; Revelation 19:13). This title is something of a mystery to English readers when they first come to the Bible. As a title it had affinities with similar words related to God (or the gods) in Middle Eastern culture and among Greek speakers as well. It was the kind of word or phrase that alerted the reader that something "divine" was in the air when it was used.[1] Each religion or culture filled it with its own ideas, and that also was true of Christianity. To discover what it meant, then, we must see how John uses it. When we do that we may say the following: the "Word" refers to God's self-expression

This essay first appeared in *Reformation & Revival Journal*, 9, No. 4 (Fall 2000), 13–22.

in his Son in such a way that the Son both is God and yet does not exhaust God. He has the very nature of God, but the Word can be distinguished from both Father and Spirit.

Second, in its usual sense as speech or writing, the Word of God would include everything that God has ever said at any time and at any place in heaven or in earth. Of most of this we are totally ignorant. Assuming that he speaks to the elect angels, we know almost nothing of what he has said. The same is true of what he says to Satan and his forces. Yet in both cases what God said and says could certainly be called the Word of God.[2]

Third, this leads to the important point that for us the Word of God must be limited to what he has revealed to us in the Bible. This is not to deny that God works through our minds and judgments to convey his will. Nor do we deny that we receive impulses that are, in fact, from him. There is, however, an enormously important distinction to be made when we compare his activity within us with his written revelation. We are sure that his Word is inerrant; we have no such assurance concerning our minds, our judgments, or our impulses. Only the Bible, properly interpreted, provides certainty.

With these facts as a backdrop for our discussion let us sharpen our focus a bit with a question: What is it about the Bible that can be properly called the Word of God?

THE BIBLE AND ITS WORDS

For many, the answer to this question is easy. The Word of God and the words of the Bible are the same thing. But that answer simply moves us to ask, "What words?" There are a multitude of Bible translations and their words do not agree. Which translation, then, contains the right words? Is it the New International Version (NIV), the New King James Version (NKJV), the New Revised Standard Version (NRSV), or some other? You see the problem: If the words and the Word are identical, then which set of words must we choose?

A frequent answer to this question and, in one sense, a profoundly true answer, is this: The original Hebrew and Greek words make up the Word of God. The difficulty with this answer is obvious to most of us. The typical Christian does not read Greek and Hebrew. What about him or her? Even if he did, how could he convey the Word of God to others who had not learned the languages? Must a man or a woman become a linguist to be saved—salvation by academic achievement? That might be a gospel for a handful of scholars, but not for the rest of us! Clearly we are on the wrong track here.

I said above, however, that there is a profoundly true sense in which the Hebrew and Greek words make up the Word of God. What I meant was this. Those words (along with some Aramaic in the Old Testament) are the words inspired by God. That is tremendously important, yet even that is subject to easy misunderstanding. To see what I mean, step back from the words for a moment and think instead of the *content* of those words, the points they convey. Suppose that is the focus of the doctrine of inspiration, what then?

Let me tell you a true story that will illustrate what I mean. Some years ago a man visited the church where I am a pastor. He told me that he had previously visited a nearby church and asked what they knew about our church. The pastor said that he did not know a whole lot about us, but he knew that we did not preach the Word of God! (Talk about an awesome indictment! It tempts me to turn aside and tell you not to ask one church about another. But I refrain!)

You may have guessed by now that the other pastor was not happy with our choice of translations. It appears that he thought the words of the King James Version (KJV) were inspired and the words of other translations were not. Perhaps he was right and I was wrong. At least some people think this is worth arguing about. The fact is, however, I might have turned his own argument against him. We could not have settled the question of which translation was the inspired Word of God. That would have been too tough for fellows like us. But I could have pointed out that if we must use inspired words in our preaching, the only way he could meet his own criterion would be for him to recite the King James Version and add absolutely no words of his own when he preached. Otherwise he would have been just like me—preaching something other than the Word of God! If the words and the Word of God are the same things, then recitation is the only way to "preach" the Word of God. Is that what he did? I suspect not.

The answer to our problem lies in this fact: We are not primarily interested in the words themselves but in their *content*, the truth they contain. Notice the word *primarily* in the previous sentence. Let me tell you why it is important. The words in the original languages were there to convey content or truth. If you and I know and embrace that truth, then we know and embrace God's Word. It makes no difference whatsoever what words were used to convey it to us, and it makes no difference what words we use to convey it to others. If the words we use accurately convey the content of Scripture, that is all that is necessary. *The content is the Word of God.* That is why the phrase "the Word of God" is sometimes replaced by the word *truth*.[3] The focus in both cases is on content not words.

What about the original words, then? They act as a standard against which everything that claims to be the Word of God must be measured. It is not necessary that you and I be able to apply that standard ourselves, that is, to read the original languages. Ruling out versions that have been done by single translators, I feel confident in saying that any of the committee versions (if you ignore their footnotes!) adequately convey the Word of God, that is, the truths contained in the original manuscripts.[4] Our conclusion for this section is as follows: Those who use the committee versions of the Bible have little to worry about in following their lead. They have in their hands the Word of God.

THE RELATION OF WORDS AND MEANINGS

But we are not yet done.

The other basic point that you must grasp is this: Generally speaking, individual words have no meanings, or rather, they have so many meanings that you cannot glance at them and know what they mean. Take the word *cut*, for example. What does it mean? The dictionary at my desk—by no means an exhaustive dictionary—gives ninety-two definitions for the word *cut*.[5] What conclusion shall we draw from this? Communication is impossible? Not at all! (If it were, you would have stopped reading this book long before now.)

The proper conclusion is this: Words in groups have meanings. Context (phrases, clauses, sentences, paragraphs, books) determines what a word means. We understand this instinctively. I listed in the previous sentence some things that constitute context, but I could easily add to that list. For example, social context is very important. "Murder the bums!" means one thing at a baseball game and something entirely different in gang warfare. Is all this overwhelming? Not really. We do not often think about it, but subconsciously we sort out these kinds of things every day; and we usually get them right.

As Bible students, however, we need to pursue this matter of meaning and context further. For some years we have insisted upon what is called "verbal inspiration," a phrase that is accurate enough in a way but is often both ridiculed and misunderstood. Those who have ridiculed it have often said something like this: "The thoughts of the Bible were inspired but not the words." For years this passed as a plausible criticism of verbal inspiration in some circles, but of course it was nothing of the kind. If we speak of the inspiration of the Bible at all, we have to be speaking of its words. A typical Bible is made up of ink and paper combined in such a way as to give us words and sentences. Can we speak of the inspiration of the ink or paper? Not if we want anyone to take us seriously! What is left? The words (and the sentences they form). If the Bible is inspired, it is the words that are inspired. The only access we have to the thoughts of the writers and of God are the words. Inspiration, if it exists at all, is bound to be *verbal*.

This, I think, is universally recognized these days. No one could accuse the liberal theologian, James Barr, of conservative bias, so we will let him make the point for us:

[The Bible's] linguistic form, far from being something anti-thetical to its "real meaning," is the means by which the meaning is conveyed; it is the criterion by which we test all interpretations which claim to state the meaning. The basic principle of interpretation is: Why was it said in this way, and not in some other way? The linguistic form of the text is not a jumble of dead symbols from which by some process of decipherment meaning has to be extracted; it is the expression of meaning....This being so...we no longer have any good reason to be shy about including a reference to the verbal form of the Bible in any assertions we make about its status as a whole....What we know about the authors, the ideas, the inner theology and so on is known ultimately from the verbal form of the Bible.[6]

This truth, however, has led to distortion and misunderstanding in another way. It has led Bible-believers to put undue stress on its words individually rather than as parts of sentences and the larger context. Many a Bible study and sermon has been made up primarily of word studies. Of course, we who preach and teach must know the meanings of the words in the Bible, but we must also recognize that when we have looked up those words in a dictionary we have simply learned what they *may mean* in their context, not what they *do mean*. If they are to be experienced as the Word of God and not simply as words, we must understand them as sentences and para-graphs, etc. To put it another way, the Word of God is found in the combinations of words the Bible contains. The Word of God is the content and the truth conveyed by those combinations. Concentrating on individual words distorts the meaning of Scripture and keeps us from understanding it. On the other hand, recognition of this fact works for the good of all of us who read the text. Let me show you how.

In Luke 20:10 the word *produce* appears. (Humour me here and pronounce the word *produce* to yourself right now.) If we consult our dictionary it will, in effect, ask us whether we want to know the meaning of the noun or the verb. Without the verse in front of you, however, you probably do not know which it is. But if you said it to yourself a moment ago when I asked you to, you made up your mind without any evidence! If you pronounced it with emphasis on the first syllable ("pro-"), you unconsciously opted for the noun which often means something like "farm products." If you pronounced it with emphasis on the second syllable ("-duce"), you unconsciously opted for the verb, which often means "to manufacture" or "to make." See how helpless you are without a context! That is the way we all are if we treat words as isolated entities. In that case we need an enormous amount of help.

But the situation changes dramatically when we add the surrounding words. Even a single sentence makes an enormous difference. Here is the sentence that the word *produce* appears in. "When the season came, he sent a slave to the tenants in order that they might give him his share of the produce of the vineyard; but the tenants beat him and sent him away empty-handed." That is much better! Depending on how familiar you are with the Bible a great deal more context may flood your mind. In fact, a whole parable and much of its meaning may already have come to mind as you read this.

Let me try to show you the significance of this little exercise that you have just gone through. It has often worried me that there seem to be so many layers of "experts" or scholars that fall between me and the meaning of the text. After all, was the Bible not written for ordinary people in ordinary jobs faced with the ordinary difficulties of life? Surely the answer is yes; that was exactly God's intention in giving it to us, to make it accessible to all kinds of people. And here is the point: Contextual reading of the Scripture makes its major points accessible—humanly speaking—to all kinds of men, women and children once they have it in their own language. The more you read, the more you will learn.

Does that mean we do not need the "experts" at all? Not quite. Language groups without the Scriptures are still at an immense handicap; they need linguists and preachers very badly indeed. This ought to remind us, however, that ultimately the understanding and embracing of Scripture depends on the work of God. Do you remember the words of the Lord Jesus when he spoke of the "harvest," that is, the progress of Christian work, as having a Lord who controls it for his purposes (Matthew 9:38)? That means that whether any person hears it or not depends on God. It also means that once a man or woman has heard it whether they understand it or not also depends on the work of God. We need him to send us his word through his agents, but for most of us in the Western world he has already done that. We also need his Spirit to make us to understand what we read, but believers have the Spirit of God (Romans 8:9). Beyond that our scholars and pastors can help us greatly. None of us is self-sufficient. God has made us, however, capable of learning the Scriptures for ourselves if we will concentrate primarily on portions much larger than single words.

SUMMING UP

I have tried in this chapter to bring home to you two major points. First, the phrase "the Word of God" is used in two distinct ways in Scripture. In a few cases it is a name or title given to the second person of the Trinity, God the Son. Its major use, however, is as a description of the Bible itself. We may say with full conviction, "the Bible is the Word of God." When the Lord Jesus met Satan in the wilderness, Jesus said, "One does not live by bread alone, but by every word that comes from the mouth of God" (Matthew 4:4). We see what he meant by this when we note that he was quoting Scripture when he said this (Deuteronomy 8:3). Beyond that, he followed each of Satan's temptations by quoting more Scripture that applied to himself. "The word" and the Scripture proved to be the same thing in this case.

Second, we learned that the Word of God is the truth or the content of Scripture. That does not mean that the words are unimportant, not at all! It does mean, however, that if we focus on larger units like sentences and paragraphs we will learn what Scripture means more rapidly and with less likelihood of distortion. It is the context and the combinations of words that convey the truths that God wants us to take in. Occasionally we will run across a word that needs attention on its own because it is unfamiliar to us or because it is used in some technical sense. But that is unusual, because the Scriptures were written for ordinary people and because excellent translations in our own language are available to us.

Christians, then, must take heart as they face the text of Scripture. Every once in a while we become discouraged when we listen to a pastor or scholar explain one word or a small phrase from "the original." It seems we have to be linguists after all to grasp God's Word! But keep this in mind: However true the scholar's explanation of that small part is, the great themes of Scripture are open to all. That means, assuming you are a believer, with the Spirit of God, they are open to you. You must not despise the learning of others. Listen to them and learn. But do not be intimidated. Scripture belongs to all of God's people. If you are one of those, it is yours to read and to know.

2

THE PERSON OF CHRIST
AS THE WORK OF CHRIST

Despite TV's recent interest in angels, the Bible treats recognizable angelic visits as rare. A visit from an angel was big news. You could not predict such a visit and, presumably, you could not forget it. It is probably due to Mary's memory, then, that we have the following from the lips of the angel Gabriel: "The Holy Spirit will come upon you, and the power of the Most High will overshadow you; and for that reason the holy offspring shall be called the Son of God" (Luke 1:35).

In the Bible we find more than one person or group seen as the son or sons of God. It may be that the godly line of Seth bears this title (Genesis 6:2). To God in Egypt Israel was "My son, My first-born." So he said to Pharaoh, "Let my son go, that he may serve me" (Exodus 4:22–23). Pharaoh refused and quickly learned how much God loved his son. The angels too are God's sons (Job 1:6), as are Christians today (2 Corinthians 6:16–18; compare 7:1). The phrase "son of God" has many and varied uses.

This essay first appeared in *Reformation & Revival Journal*, 8, No. 4 (Fall 1999), 91–105.

The early chapters of Luke contain yet another use of this phrase. In the genealogy of Jesus we read of "Adam, the *son* of God" (Luke 3:38). Luke looks on Adam's creation at the hand of God as sonship to God himself. The reason is not hard to find. At Adam's creation he was made to be (or bear) "the image of God" (Genesis 1:26–27). Given his responsibilities (Genesis 1:28–30), we may judge that this "image" was the ability to govern the rest of creation and the character necessary to do so. In large measure Adam lost these very things when he sinned.

It is against the backdrop of Adam's sin that the Lord Jesus appears as "the Son of God." The Psalmist sings in a major key of man's exalted office in creation: "Thou has made him a little lower than the angels, and dost crown him with glory and majesty! …Thou hast put all things under his feet…" (Psalm 8:5–6). But the writer to the Hebrews weighs in with a sombre minor: "But now we do not yet see all things subjected to him" (Hebrews 2:8). Not quite a sour note, but gloomy nevertheless! Sin robbed man of his glory! Yet that is not the whole story. Our Lord Jesus has entered the scene as the Son of God who will make the Psalmist's prophetic word come to pass.

It is usual to discuss the Lord Jesus Christ under two headings, the person of Christ and the work of Christ. His person, of course, is who he was and is, whereas his work is what he did and does. This division is sensible and has been widely used. But in one respect the two themes overlap. Who he was on earth was part of the work he was sent to do. Put another way, his character was a revelation of what God is like. Showing what God is like was a prime part of his work. I have entitled this chapter *The person of Christ as the work of Christ* for that reason.

The Lord Jesus, then, came to display the character of God, to show what God is like. Of course he did this through the media of his words and work, but those who saw his deeds and heard his teaching soon discovered something else. He was not simply the conduit through which these good things arrived. He himself was more than the sum of his activities. An eyewitness said, "We beheld his glory," and described it as "glory as of the only begotten of the Father, full of grace and truth" (John 1:14). How could this be? Jesus explained it this way: "He who has seen me has seen the Father" (John 14:9). In his humanity, the character of God was so deeply impressed on him that it was as really his as the act of breathing. Do you remember what the temple police said? "Never did a man speak the way this man speaks" (John 7:46). Their witness was true because there never was such a man as this man was.

WHAT THEN WAS JESUS LIKE?

To begin with, we must understand the question. In describing Jesus we talk about how he is like God in what have been called God's *communicable attributes*. That means that he was like God in those things that God can share with others. There are some things God cannot share with mere men: his omnipresence, for instance, his ability to be everywhere at once. There is his omniscience, his knowledge of everything. There is also his eternity, his existence as far back and as far forward as one can conceive; and you may think of others.[1]

There are things that God can share with men. They include God's moral character and other things as well. These things did not simply pass through the Lord Jesus from God to us. They were natively his as a man. When the Lord Jesus walked the earth, he walked it as a man. When he was tested, he was tested as a man. When he rejoiced, he rejoiced as a man rejoices; when he wept, he wept as a man weeps. In each case, these actions were the actions of a man. They were really his actions as a man, but they revealed the very character of God.

Someone may say, "Did Jesus not display omniscience and omnipotence as well?" and "Were these things not native to him as God?" These are good questions. I think the answer to both is yes, but I think something else also. For most of his life on earth, perhaps for all of it, Jesus limited the exercise of his attributes as God. That is why he could say of the time of his return, "But of that day and hour no one knows, not even the angels of heaven, nor the

Son, but the Father alone" (Matthew 24:36). He did things that only God could do, but he did them, not by his own power but by the power of the Spirit. Even in John's gospel where this might seem less evident, it remains true. "For he whom God has sent speaks the words of God, for [God] gives the Spirit [to Him] without measure. The Father loves the Son, and has given all things into his hand" (John 3:34–35).[2] The presence of the Spirit accounts for whatever superhuman work he does and whatever superhuman qualities he shows. We will pass over these things and seek instead some qualities of God that Jesus revealed as the preeminent man among men.

THE WISDOM OF CHRIST

Biblical wisdom is skill for living especially in the choice and pursuit of goals. The earliest reference to what the Lord Jesus was like in his mental and moral life is found in Luke: "And the Child continued to grow and become strong, *increasing in wisdom*; and the grace of God was upon him.…And Jesus kept *increasing* in wisdom and stature, and in favor with God and men" (Luke 2:40,52, *italics added*). Luke twice remarks on the wisdom of Christ at an age when we do not usually credit people with wisdom. Yet Luke speaks of his literally "being filled with wisdom" (Luke 2:40). No doubt this refers to a fullness consistent with the capacity of a boy his age, since in verse 52 he increases in wisdom as he grows up. These verses bracket the incident in which the Lord Jesus stayed behind at the temple while his parents started home after Passover. Luke brings out the depth of his wisdom in the apparently stray remark that his parents "did not understand the statement which he made to them" in explaining why he had stayed behind (Luke 2:50). Why didn't they understand? Not through any lack of clarity in Jesus' statement, but because of his deeper insight into his role in life, even at that young age.

The early signs of wisdom in Jesus no doubt contributed to Luke's remark that he increased "in favor with…men" (Luke 2:52). In his public ministry, however, things changed. His wisdom, now increased in keeping with his adult capacity, did not keep him from getting mixed reviews. We see this in Nazareth. The initial reaction to his teaching was astonishment. "Where did this man get this wisdom, and these miraculous powers?" (Matthew 13:54) They had known him and his family all their lives. He could not be anyone special! "And they took offense at him" (Matthew 13:57).

As his ministry proceeded, his wisdom was set loose on the enemies of God, and they smarted under it. Plans to trap him were cleverly laid, but they regularly failed. Human ingenuity was no match for the wisdom of Christ, a wisdom informed by the purposes of God. His enemies floundered while he steadily pursued the will of God. When the time came for him to be "lifted up," in their ignorance they fell in with God's plan. "Away with Him," they cried, "away with Him, crucify Him!" (John 19:15) In so doing, they were the blind instruments the Father used in answering the prayer of Wisdom incarnate: "My Father, if this cannot pass away unless I drink it, Thy will be done" (Matthew 26:42). The career the Lord Jesus wisely pursued, including the cross and the resurrection, is a transparent proof of the wisdom of God.

THE FAITHFULNESS OF CHRIST

Faithfulness, in God, means being true to his word. In man it means being true both to his own word and to his responsibilities. The plan of God to turn us back to himself depended jointly on God's faithfulness and the faithfulness of Jesus. In his evident faithfulness, the Lord Jesus set the faithfulness of God before our eyes.

We have seen that, in some ways, the knowledge of Jesus was limited. No one can say when the full horror of his destiny fell across his mind. Did he know at age twelve or at age thirty? We have no basis for even a guess. It is clear, however, that the backdrop of eventual death lay behind his activity almost from the beginning of his public ministry. When Satan said of the kingdoms of this world, "All these things will I give You if You fall down and worship me" (Matthew 4:9), did he mean Jesus to see an easier path—easier than the cross—to lordship over this world?

Given the wisdom of Jesus, his Father's plan must have become plain to him not later than the early months of his ministry. In chapter two of Mark's Gospel it is already suggested *to us* in the hostility he arouses. Beyond that, he speaks of days "when the bridegroom is taken away from" his attendants (Mark 2:20). What can this mean, except his death by violence?

The exact time is not the central issue. At some point in the years before his crucifixion, God's plan lay open before his mind. The effect was this: From then on, an incessant clamour for faithfulness on his part rang in his ears. In one sense that was his only responsibility. It is instructive to see how he met it.

To begin with, he often reminded himself of why he came, why he existed as man. He did this in two ways. First he spoke in general terms of coming to do God's will. When he was urged to eat he said, "I have food to eat that you do not know about" (John 4:32). He enjoyed the mental excitement of pondering and doing the will of God. So he added, "My food is to do the will of Him who sent Me, and to accomplish His work" (John 4:34; compare John 6:38; Hebrews 10:9). Second, he spelled out exactly what the will of God meant: "[T]he Son of Man did not come to be served, but to serve, and to give His life a ransom for many" (Matthew 20:28). Both generally and explicitly he contemplated his end.

But that could not be all. Reaching goals takes much more than thinking on them. Preliminary steps must be taken. In Jesus' case this was complicated by a timetable. He could not, in one exuberant burst of physical and moral energy, bring himself to the cross. Yes, he had authority to lay down his life (John 10:18), but only on the strictest schedule. He could have given himself up to the temple police (John 7:35–36), but no, it was not time. He could have allowed himself to be taken at the treasury, but "no one seized Him, because His hour had not yet come" (John 8:20; compare John 7:30).

Even at the end, he required faithfulness. It cost him anguish in the garden (Luke 22:44), restraint at his arrest (Matthew 26:52–54), plain speech before the Jewish leaders (Luke 22:66–71), bearing false accusation before Pilate (Luke 23:2) and silence before Herod

(Luke 23:9). Nor was that all! On the cross, he faced the temptation of his abusers, "[S]ave Yourself! If You are the Son of God, come down from the cross" (Matthew 27:40).

What do we learn from the faithfulness of Jesus? Though he was a man, he teaches us the faithfulness of God. Here again, his person was his work.

THE RIGHTEOUSNESS OF CHRIST

Righteousness, in God, is his devotion to what is right and just. Men too are said to be righteous when they share that same devotion.[3] When we meet the ideas of righteousness and justice in Scripture, they often savour of the lawcourt. In the earliest explicit mention of God's righteousness, Abraham addresses God as Judge: "Far be it from Thee to do such a thing, to slay the righteous with the wicked, so that the righteous and the wicked are treated alike. Far be it from Thee! Shall not the Judge of all the earth deal justly [do right]?" (Genesis 18:25).

God made man morally pure, and he was pleased with him. That pleasure was part of the larger satisfaction he found in all he made. Scripture says, "God saw all that He had made, and behold, it was very good" (Genesis 1:31). The fall, however, changed things. Man and creation remained "good" in the sense that they still served the purposes of God, but a new purpose became evident. The element of evil in the world had to be dealt with, and God had to do so in a righteous way. The alternative would have been the full destruction of mankind. So God planned for a righteous sufferer, our Lord Jesus, who would die as a substitute for sinners.

Was the Lord Jesus a righteous man? We need only look at him to find the answer.

We first see the evidence of his righteousness in his sinless life. At the outset of his public ministry this sinlessness is implied in the rigorous contest with Satan. Why else concentrate all the forces of wickedness on Jesus? What was the result? Clearly, Jesus was as innocent after this battle as he was before. Unlike the rest of us, the consciousness of innocence was his continually. Describing himself, he said, "He who speaks from himself seeks his own glory; but He who is seeking the glory of the one who sent Him, He is true, and there is no unrighteousness in Him" (John 7:18). No unrighteousness!

In John 8:44–47, we find illustrated his sense of separation from sinners:

> You are of your father the devil, and you want to do the desires of your father. He was a murderer from the beginning, and does not stand in the truth, because there is no truth in him. Whenever he speaks a lie, he speaks from his own nature; for he is a liar, and the father of lies. But because I speak the truth, you do not believe Me. Which one of you convicts Me of sin? If I speak the truth, why do you not believe Me? He who is of God hears the words of God; for this reason you do not hear them, because you are not of God.

It is clear that Jesus puts his listeners in a category distinct from his own. They are Satan's children; he is not. They believe lies; he speaks truth. They are not of God; he is. He protests his innocence: "Which one of you convicts Me of sin?" He expects no answer, and receives none! They ask a question that contains this slander: "You are a Samaritan and have a demon" (John 8:48), but, as to sin, they are silent. "Moral indignation must be accompanied by confession of sin in anyone else," yet there is no trace of consciousness of sin here![4] We recognize, of course, how easy it is to protest our own innocence. But when such words come from the lips of the greatest moral teacher who ever lived, they carry a weight that amounts to certainty. Of Jesus we can believe even this, spoken on the night of his arrest: "[T]he ruler of the world is coming, *and he has nothing in Me*" (John 14:30, *italics added*).

We see the righteousness of the Lord Jesus in another way, his acceptance with God. Which of us could pray as he prayed at Lazarus' tomb?

And Jesus raised His eyes, and said, "Father, I thank Thee that Thou heardest Me. And I knew that Thou hearest Me always..." And when He had said these things, He cried out with a loud voice, "Lazarus, come forth." He who had died came forth, bound hand and foot with wrappings...Jesus said to them, "Unbind him, and let him go" (John 11:41–44).

How often did the Father hear him? "Always." How do we know? "He who had died came forth."

There is yet a greater act of acceptance on his Father's part, the acceptance of his sacrifice authenticated by his resurrection from the dead. God himself described this acceptance through Isaiah centuries before he came:

As a result of the anguish of His soul, He will see it and be satisfied; By His knowledge the Righteous One, My Servant, will justify many, As He will bear their iniquities. Therefore, I will allot Him a portion with the great, And He will divide the booty with the strong; Because He poured out Himself to death, and was numbered with the transgressors...(Isaiah 53:11–12).

How Jesus could receive "a portion with the great" and "booty with the strong" after his death becomes clear in the account of his resurrection, God's stamp of approval on his person and work.

Finally, we see his righteousness stressed by his first-century followers. In preaching shortly after Pentecost, Peter calls him "the Holy and Righteous One" (Acts 3:14). In his first epistle he describes Jesus as having committed "no sin, nor was any deceit found in His mouth" (1 Peter 2:22). Paul speaks of him as the one "who knew no sin" (2 Corinthians 5:21). The writer of Hebrews speaks of Jesus as "one who has been tempted in all things as we are, yet without sin" (Hebrews 4:15) and describes him as "holy, innocent [and] undefiled" (Hebrews 7:26). He also reminds us that unlike the Levitical priests he had no need to offer sacrifice for his own sins (Hebrews 7:27). John says plainly, "He is righteous" (1 John 2:29) and "in Him there is no sin" (1 John 3:5).

It was necessary that Jesus was a righteous man in order to be God's righteous sufferer. It was also necessary to properly display the character of his Father.

THE ANGER OR WRATH OF CHRIST

Wrath is the reaction of a righteous moral being against sin and ungodliness. It was and is closely related to righteousness in the Lord Jesus. It is the necessary evidence that righteousness was more than a mere name in him. B.B. Warfield has written:

> The moral sense is not a mere faculty of discrimination between the qualities which we call right and wrong...[It passes] moral judgments; that is to say, they involve approval and disapproval...It would be impossible, therefore, for a moral being to stand in the presence of perceived wrong, indifferent and unmoved. Precisely what we mean by a moral being is a being perceptive of the difference between right and wrong and reacting appropriately...The emotions of indignation and anger belong therefore to the very self-expression of a moral being as such and cannot be lacking to him in the presence of wrong.[5]

The experience of Jesus bears this out. Anger or wrath was part of his life. We meet it when he sees the Jewish leaders hostile to himself and indifferent to the man with the withered hand. "Is it lawful on the Sabbath," he asked, "to do good...?" (Mark 3:4) The question was met with sullen silence to which Jesus reacted strongly. He looked "at them with anger, grieved by their hardness of heart..." (Mark 3:5). Considering the woes that he pronounced on these kinds of men, he must have often felt moral indignation at their coldness. A single chapter in Matthew contains the phrase, "Woe to you, scribes and Pharisees, hypocrites," six or seven times (Matthew 23:13–29).[6] These "woes" do not simply reflect sorrow.

They reflect the anger of Jesus at the abuse of religion by the Jewish leaders. His choice of the words "fools" (Matthew 23:17), "serpents" and "brood of vipers" (Matthew 23:33) to describe them did not arise from pity, but from outrage.

Yet in all of this, the man Christ Jesus exhibits the attitudes of his Father. The humanity of Jesus reflects the moral image of God. It will continue to do so in the future. That is why we meet the surprising phrase, "the wrath of the Lamb" (Revelation 6:16), near the end of the New Testament.

THE LOVE OF CHRIST

Love is an affection that leads one to seek the benefit, or promote the interest, of another. Looked on by some as the central attribute of God's nature, love abounded in the life of our Saviour.

It is clear that the Lord Jesus loved men generally. We see this love in his acts of compassion. Many of these were done to individuals who might well have been among his elect (Matthew 20:34; Mark 1:41), but that is not the whole story. His compassion extended to mixed multitudes. The feeling of compassion led him into various acts of love for large groups. He directed his disciples to prayer because of his compassion for multitudes (Matthew 9:36–38). Repeatedly he healed multitudes of sick (Matthew 14:14; Luke 4:40). His compassion led him to feed a multitude (Matthew 15:32), and in a vivid witness to what is strategically important he *taught* a multitude of five thousand men, plus women and children (Mark 6:34,44).

God's elect were special objects of his love. John makes this plain in recounting the story of his final hours. Jesus said, "Greater love has no one than this, that one lays down his life for his friends" (John 15:12). Who are these friends? "You are My friends, if you do what I command you" (John 15:14). We must not understand this to mean that they became his friends by their obedience. That would overthrow grace and throw all of us who know our own sinfulness into despair. No, they were friends because he befriended them and chose them out of the world (John 15:19). All they were could be traced to his love, the love of his Father and the love of the Spirit, that special love that belongs to all his elect people.

Finally, two closely related loves lived in the breast of Jesus: love for the Father and love for the truth the Father revealed. This led to his fulfilling the first and greatest commandment, to love "God with all your heart, and with all your soul and with all your mind" (Matthew 22:37).

At first glance, we might think that love for the Father and love for truth are appropriate to creatures but could hardly portray the interior life of God. But even here the Lord Jesus reflects God's image. It would not be meaningful to describe God as "love" (1 John 4:8,16) unless that description had always been true. We are not to think of growth and development in God, as though he were a creature. It is true that love for men generally and love for his elect always existed in God; in that sense he always loved. But there was an even higher sense, a logically prior sense, in which God exercised love in eternity past. The persons of the Trinity loved one another. Father loved Son and Spirit. The Son loved the Father and the Spirit. The Spirit loved both Father and Son.[7] In loving one another they loved one another's characters, including the attribute of truth.

The love, then, that we find in Christ mirrors the makeup of the God who sent him.

SUMMING UP

In writing to the Colossians, Paul portrayed the Lord Jesus in these words: "He is the image of the invisible God, the firstborn of all creation" (Colossians 1:15). Again, he spoke of "the glory of Christ, who is the image of God" (2 Corinthians 4:4). The writer to the Hebrews adopted similar language: "He is the radiance of His glory and the exact representation of His nature" (Hebrews 1:3). These sweeping statements cannot be confined to the humanity of the Lord Jesus; they describe humanity and deity in the unique God-man. To discuss their broad reach is beyond us. Our aim has been more modest, to look on Christ at the level most accessible to us, his simple humanity.

And what did we find? We found in him the character of his Father. It does not pass through him to us as if he were a conduit, unaffected by what he carries. Not at all! What we see is himself. He displays the nature of God by sharing the nature of God in his humanity. The communicable (shareable) attributes of God are his own attributes. In that way, his person is his work.

3

MADE LIKE
HIS BROTHERS

The past century was a difficult century. Wars and rumours of wars were rampant; earthquakes and other natural disasters took their toll worldwide. In addition, print and broadcast media brought these things to our attention in ways once undreamed of.

The theological world has been shaken by wars and earthquakes of its own. The twentieth century, for example, saw the blossoming of modernism, a movement noted for its abandonment of the doctrine of the full deity of Jesus Christ. Much of fundamentalism and evangelicalism was shaped by reaction to that denial. When the battle lines were drawn on this issue, each side took the stance it thought to be the most useful in defending Christian doctrine as it understood it. Conservatives are what they are, to an important degree, because modernists advertised their faith in the humanity of Jesus Christ at the expense of his deity.

But there is an odd fact about that battle: Through much of church history it would have seemed necessary to side with the

This essay first appeared in *Reformation & Revival Journal*, 2, No. 2 (Spring 1993), 45–54.

modernists (had they been around) in asserting that Jesus Christ is fully and truly man. It may be that the humanity of Jesus Christ has come under attack even more often than his deity.

At the end of the first century, Christians confronted an error called Docetism. The word comes from a Greek verb meaning "to seem" or "to appear." The Docetists contended that Christ seemed to be man, he appeared human, but his humanity was just that: an appearance. They said this because they thought that human flesh, along with all other matter, was evil. In their own mistaken way, they hope to preserve the purity of Christ by denying that his flesh was real. Such a notion, however, would have been fatal to true Christianity if it had carried the day.

It seems likely that John addressed this problem in his first epistle. He wrote of false prophets:

> This is how you can recognize the Spirit of God: Every spirit that acknowledges that Jesus Christ has come in the flesh is from God, but every spirit that does not acknowledge Jesus is not from God. This is the spirit of antichrist…(1 John 4:2–3a).

And again in his second epistle he wrote: "Many deceivers, who do not acknowledge Jesus Christ as coming in the flesh, have gone out into the world. Any such person is the deceiver and the antichrist" (2 John 7). These harsh words show how strongly the Spirit of God, speaking through John, felt about Docetism. To deny that Jesus Christ was fully human was the work of antichrist and not of God. We may note in passing that Mary Baker Eddy's Christian Science, by denying the reality of matter, falls under the condemnation of Scripture at this point.

The fourth and fifth centuries saw the development of Monophysitism ("one-naturism"), a serious attempt to do justice to the deity of Christ, that endangered the doctrine of his full humanity. The Monophysites did not deny that Jesus' flesh was real, but their doctrine of only one nature in Christ threatened his true humanity. If our Lord had only the nature of God or a composite nature that was a mixture of humanity and divinity, how could he be truly human? To their opponents the Monophysites made Christ appear to be God dressed up in human flesh merely to look like a man.

Docetism and Monophysitism were fairly straightforward attacks on Christ's humanity. Later centuries added others that were more subtle. In the thirteenth century the Roman Catholic Church adopted the view that the human body of the Lord Jesus replaced the bread and wine of the communion service. To the eye and to the tongue of the worshipper bread and wine seemed to be present, but in fact his senses deceived him. What he was eating and drinking were the literal flesh and blood of Jesus. What's wrong with this? It demands a question: Are we dealing here with a real and true human body if it can be everywhere in the world at once? To many, the answer seems to be, No. Yet at the Reformation, Martin Luther adopted an understanding of the Lord's table that demanded the same quality of ubiquity—the ability of Christ's body to be everywhere at once. A natural retort to this criticism might be: "The body of the risen Jesus passed through doors that were not open, yet we do not deny the reality of his human flesh on that account. Why then question the ability of his flesh to be everywhere at once?" Still, uneasiness remains, in part because one can imagine our own glorified bodies with unusual properties, but not with the quality of being everywhere at once.

More serious yet was the doctrine of some of the sixteenth-century Anabaptists. They said and wrote that Christ's flesh was heavenly flesh. They meant by this that nothing of Mary's humanity was passed on to her son. The humanity of Jesus, like his deity, came to him from heaven. In their view, Mary acted only as the container in which the Lord Jesus spent the first nine months of his existence. She contributed nothing of herself to his human life. Critics of this view, however, have seen that a humanity that has nothing in common with Mary (and hence with Adam) is not true humanity at all.

Yet Jesus Christ was and is truly man, and the Scriptures make this point in many ways.

The earliest prophecy of the coming of Christ speaks of him as the offspring of Eve, the first mother of humanity. As part of the curse on the serpent God says: "And I will put enmity between you and the woman, and between your offspring and hers; he will crush your head, and you will strike His heel" (Genesis 3:15). Nothing in this prophecy suggests Christ's deity. Clearly the offspring of the woman would be a man. More than that, the fact that the serpent or Satan would "strike His heel" shows his vulnerability, a prominent human trait. It is not of God but of man that Job says, "Man born of woman is of few days and full of trouble" (Job 14:1). The "striking" of the Messiah's heel would prove to be trouble of the severest kind.

Later prophecies, of course, asserted or suggested that the Messiah or Christ would be God. But even these mentioned his humanity. Look at Isaiah 9:6: "For to us a child is born, to us a Son is given, and the government will be on His shoulders. And He will be called Wonderful Counselor, Mighty God, Everlasting Father, Prince of Peace." The one who will come as Mighty God and Everlasting Father will be born as a human babe, a son of man. We find the same thing in Micah 5:2: "But you, Bethlehem Ephrathah, though you are small among the clans of Judah, out of you will come for Me one who will be ruler over Israel, whose origins are from old, from ancient times." The reference to Christ's origins—"from old, from ancient times," or as the margin reads, "from days of eternity"—is probably an indication of his deity. But it does not stand alone. Here also is the place of his birth as a king from the line of David, as a human child.

When we turn to the New Testament, we find the same interest in the true humanity of our Lord. The birth narratives in Matthew and Luke speak for themselves. Not only does the actual birth bear witness to the humanity of our Saviour, but the announcement of the angel speaks of "a baby wrapped in cloths and lying in a manger" (Luke 2:12). A baby!—a baby that grows up (Luke 2:40,52) and as a man hungers (Luke 4:2) and thirsts (John 4:7) and grows weary (John 4:6) and feels agony (Matthew 26:38–39) and dies (John 19:30).

The reality of Christ's humanity pervades the Bible. Behold the man! But what does it all mean? Where does its importance lie? On the most obvious level we may answer, "It proves that God is true, that what he prophesies will come to pass. The promised man-above-all-men has come, 'born of a woman' (Galatians 4:4), as God had said. Surely this is no small thing. But the main interest in the manhood of our Lord Jesus lies elsewhere. Why was he prophesied to come? And especially, why as a man?

The Bible leaves us in no doubt about the answer to these questions. No one less than the God-man could make sinful men right with a holy God. To do this, God became man. Or in the words of John 1:14, "The Word became flesh." Flesh here means more than the meat on our bones. It speaks of true humanity as in Joel's words, "I will pour out My Spirit on all people [flesh]" (quoted in Acts 2:17). Our salvation depended on Jesus Christ being man.

The writer of Hebrews makes this point:

> It is not to angels that he [God] has subjected the world to come, about which we are speaking. But there is a place where someone has testified: "What is man that You are mindful of him, the son of man that You care for him? You made Him a little lower than the angels; You crowned Him with glory and honour and put everything under His feet." In putting everything under Him, God left nothing that is not subject to Him. Yet at present we do not see everything subject to Him (Hebrews 2:5–8).

Notice two things here. First, man was promised dominion over the earth at the creation. Nothing was outside his control. Second, we cannot see man's control over all of nature. That is not because his control is invisible, but because it does not exist! The promise of God seems to have failed. What's happening here?

The writer of Hebrews goes on to answer the problem that his quotation raises:

But we see Jesus, who was made a little lower than the angels, now crowned with glory and honour because He suffered death, so that by the grace of God He might taste death for everyone. In bringing many sons to glory, it was fitting that God, for whom and through whom everything exists, should make the author of their salvation perfect through suffering (Hebrews 2:9–10).

The promise of God has not failed. Mankind does have control over all things in the person of Jesus Christ. All men are not yet crowned with honour and glory, but the representative man is. As he himself said: "All authority in heaven and on earth has been given to Me" (Matthew 28:18). The present rule of Christ is the downpayment on the promise of an earth ruled by a new nation of men and women, the new nation known as the church. When that promise is fulfilled, salvation will have come in its fullest sense. For us to be saved, Jesus Christ had to be truly man.

Yet there is more. We see it when we ask the question, "Why was Jesus crowned with glory and honour?" The answer is: "...because He suffered death, so that by the grace of God He might taste death for everyone." He was crowned because He died.

Let us explore this further. The promise made to man to rule over the earth was postponed owing to man's fall into sin. For the promise to be fulfilled, man would have to be restored to holiness. How could that be done? By the death of a substitute. The principle of substitution is pictured all through the sacrificial system of the Old Testament; but only pictured! No animal was an adequate substitute for sinful man. As the writer of Hebrews says elsewhere: "...it is impossible for the blood of bulls and goats to take away sins" (Hebrews 10:4). The only adequate substitute was a spotless human being. Since God was determined to bring "many sons to glory," he substituted the death of Jesus Christ in the place of each of those "sons" (and "daughters"). God cannot die, but the Son of God, who became a man, both could and did.

There is still more. Men often act with complex motives and

several ends in view—how much more, God! Not only did God send his son to die for sinners, he also sent him to form a family, a family of brothers:

> Both the one who makes men holy and those who are made holy are of the same family. So Jesus is not ashamed to call them brothers. He says, "I will declare Your name to My brothers; in the presence of the congregation I will sing Your praises." And again, "I will put My trust in Him." And again He says, "Here am I, and the children God has given Me." Since the children have flesh and blood, He too shared in their humanity so that by His death He might destroy him who holds the power of death—that is, the devil—and free those who all their lives were held in slavery by their fear of death. For surely it is not angels He helps, but Abraham's descendants (Hebrews 2:11–16).

The writer takes great pains to make his point. The Lord Jesus has formed a family of fellow humans. He calls them "brothers" (verses 11and 12). By trusting in God he takes his place beside them as a fellow man (verse 13). He "shares" their humanity in dying to free Abraham's descendants, literal or spiritual (verses 14–16).

Nor is all this merely formal. Not at all! The chapter closes by showing that in his death, and beyond, his acts are the acts of one who feels what his brothers and sisters feel.

> For this reason He had to be made like His brothers in every way in order that He might become a merciful and faithful high priest in service to God, and that He might make atonement for the sins of the people. Because He Himself suffered when He was tempted, He is able to help those who are being tempted (Hebrews 2:17–18).

Family membership involves family feeling. The sins and sufferings of his brothers and sisters in temptation call forth his mercy.

They need and receive the help of one who has been tempted. People receive that help, if they believe in him. In Hebrews 4 persevering faith in Christ as God and man has this promise:

> Therefore, since we have a great high priest who has gone through the heavens, Jesus the Son of God, let us hold firmly to the faith we profess. For we do not have a high priest who is unable to sympathize with our weaknesses, but we have one who has been tempted in every way, just as we are—yet was without sin. Let us then approach the throne of grace with confidence, so that we may receive mercy and find grace to help us in our time of need (Hebrews 4:14–16).

The writer's point is clear: Both for the forgiveness of our sins and for our comfort we are indebted to the humanity of Jesus Christ.

But finally, I think I hear someone saying to me, "Do you not know that you are preaching to the converted? We all believe in the true humanity of our Lord Jesus!"

Maybe—but I wonder. At the beginning of this chapter I mentioned the battle with modernism over the deity of Christ. I made the point that that battle has in some degree made us conservatives what we are. After all, we are not immune to the influences around us, secular or sacred. I wonder if the constant reiteration of the deity of our Lord has not affected us. Are we really free from the problem of the Monophysites? Do none of us think of Christ as God dressed up like a man? Do we really believe that he remains a man today and forever?

The New Testament makes it clear that the humanity of Christ is a doctrine to be believed, among other reasons, for our present comfort. Certainly it is important that we hold tenaciously to the fact that Christ is God. In the midst of a world apparently disintegrating into chaos, his control would be no more than a name if he were not God.

But the Scriptures offer us more, and we are unwise if we do not take hold of it. There is a man in heaven who knows our needs. He knows them both as God and as man. As God he knows whether they are genuine needs or mere passing lusts. As man he knows our agony and shame and sorrow. Our paramount need, according to Scripture, is just such a man; and we have him.

In closing, let me add one word of caution. If you are convinced of the full and true humanity of the Lord Jesus, it is still important how you think of him.

Do you think of him as a babe in a manger? Many do. If you join them, you will have cut him off in infancy as Herod hoped to do when he slaughtered the infants in and around Bethlehem (Matthew 2:7–18). Of what help is such a Christ to sinners like you and me?

Do you think of him as the crucifix depicts him, hanging on a cross? That is better, of course, than resigning him to perpetual babyhood. If you never visit Christ dying "outside the city gate" (Hebrews 13:12), your vision of him is deeply defective—perilously so.

If that, however, is your only vision of Jesus Christ, you may see him as needing help himself and sending you elsewhere—to ancient or modern substitutes. How many have looked on a dying Christ and turned to his blessed Mother for help? Too many, I fear! How many have celebrated his death and turned to psychology and psychiatry for daily strength? I do not know—but I have my suspicions.

The humanity of Jesus Christ is a central doctrine of the Christian faith. It does not stand alone. It cannot be set in opposition to the reality of his deity. It needs, however, its full recognition. Without it there is no atonement; without it, no present help in our time of need. We neglect it at our peril, but we celebrate it as glorious in itself and as leading us to glory and honour forever.

4

FOR WHOM DID CHRIST DIE?

Ask the average Christian the question in the title of this chapter and you are likely to get one of two reactions. Some will give you a quizzical look, as much as to say, "All right, what's the catch? Everyone knows the answer to that question." Others will say simply, "Christ died for everyone who ever lived." A small number of people will smell heresy and point an accusing finger. "Aha!" they will cry, "You are a Calvinist!" Without another word they may convey a further disheartening message: You ought to blush with shame and slink back into whatever hole it was that you crawled out of.

APPROACHING SCRIPTURE WITH PRESUPPOSITIONS

Let us take a further look at this latter reaction. A frequent complaint against Reformed or Calvinistic people goes something like this: "Your view of the atonement is not the result of Scripture but of logic. In fact, you are rationalists!" Those are harsh words indeed, but necessary, if true.

This essay first appeared in *Reformation & Revival Journal*, 5, No. 1 (Winter 1996), 51–64.

When I hear that I am a rationalist, I am reminded of something Carl F.H. Henry said in another connection: "Let those who want to defend irrationalism do it with whatever weapons they can find!" Abandon logic altogether and you must abandon all reasoned discourse. There is no discussion that does not appeal to reason from beginning to end. We have no choice. If we want to graduate from "Mama" and "Dada" we have to think in a rational way.

But to be fair, the objections really amount to this: I have a logical grid that I impress upon Scripture, and it affects how I read it. Put another way, the lens through which I look at Scripture distorts it. I do not come objectively to the Word of God. Is that really true? If it is true, is it serious?

To begin with, I must plead guilty to not being objective. It is widely recognized in our century that objectivity, however desirable it may or may not be, is not the state of any of us. We all bring a great deal of baggage to every question we seek to answer. My objector and I have this in common. What we must both do is to admit this and to keep it firmly in mind as we carry on our discussion, seeking to minimize its negative impact on us. But there is more to be said.

Let us think together about how we learn what Scripture teaches. When we come to a text that we have never carefully considered before, how shall we approach it? Sooner or later we will have to look at it in the light of all that we already know from Scripture. Of course this is virtually instinctive with us; we seldom think about what we are doing, we just do it.

To illustrate how this works, imagine that you are in a culture where Christ is not widely known and you are a relatively new Christian who has read only the four Gospels. Suppose someone tells you, "There's a verse of Scripture in Paul's letters that says quite literally that Jesus had seven arms." How will you react? You will find this difficult to believe for several reasons. The reason that interests us here is this: You have read the Gospels and have seen the reactions of men and women to the Lord Jesus. Some reacted well and others reacted violently, but none of the adverse reactions seemed to arise from his physical appearance. It is a non-issue in the Gospels. That is unthinkable if Jesus really had seven arms.

You will immediately see what happened. The baggage that you brought to this supposed verse was good baggage—the knowledge of Scripture that you already had. Your previous knowledge was imposed on the newly alleged verse. That was the lens through which you looked at it. In doing that you acted correctly. There was a danger in doing it; perhaps you misunderstood the adverse reactions of Jesus' critics. Maybe they did arise to some degree from Jesus' appearance. Maybe you needed Paul's verse to tell you that. In this hypothetical case, however, you were dead right since there is no such verse.

This demonstrates how we come to all Scripture. We bring our previous knowledge with us. What often happens is that the new Scripture is read in the light of the old, shading our understanding of the new verse, but also to a small degree correcting all that we have already held. But again, we may be hardly conscious of the process. Only if a large number of verses change our perspective appreciably will we be aware that something important is happening.

Most of us who became Christians when we were young came to Scripture with the assumption that Christ died for every person who ever lived. That is what modern evangelicalism had tended to say to us. In fact, that was the grid that we impressed on Scripture; that was the lens through which we saw it. It seemed to us inevitable that any verse that touched the atonement contained that idea either explicitly or implicitly. It was beyond question. Somewhere along the way, however, some of us changed our minds. And we thought we did it under the impact of Scripture.

SCRIPTURAL SUPPORT FOR PARTICULAR REDEMPTION

Let me share with you two points that Scripture makes repeatedly that seem to demand that Christ died only for those who are actually saved. This doctrine, by the way, is often called *limited atonement*, but I prefer to call it *particular redemption*, emphasizing the idea that Christ died for *particular* men and women. It may surprise you to know that the first mission organization involved in the modern missionary movement was called The Particular Baptist Society for propagating the Gospel among the heathen (later shortened to The Baptist Missionary Society). William Carey and those associated with him in that great effort believed that Christ died for particular people.

First, the Bible teaches that Christ died to pay the penalty of sin. This is the heart of the Reformed view. You may ask: "Do not all Christians believe that?" No, they do not. As an example, let me quote J.K. Grider in an article on "Arminianism" in the *Evangelical Dictionary of Theology*. Grider writes:

> Many Arminians whose theology is not very precise say that Christ paid the penalty for our sins. …Arminians teach that what Christ did he did for every person; therefore what he did could not have been to pay the penalty, since no one would then ever go into eternal perdition.[1]

Why did Grider say this? Because he understood the truth that was centuries earlier propounded by John Owen and others: (1) If Christ paid the penalty for every sin of every man then no man can ever suffer everlasting punishment for his own sins. His penalty has been completely borne. (2) If Christ paid the penalty for some sins of every man, then every man will have to suffer everlasting punishment for his own unpaid-for sins. (3) If Christ paid the penalty for all the sins of some men only, then only some men will be saved. (The salvation of some men only is, of course, the fact, as most of us agree.)

If we describe Christ's death in terms of paying the penalty for sins, then we will have to agree that Christ died only for those who are actually saved. That becomes clear when we look at the definition of *penalty*. According to *Funk & Wagnalls Standard College Dictionary*, a penalty is "The legal punishment for having committed a crime or having violated a law." The *Oxford Universal*

Dictionary defines a penalty as "A punishment imposed for breach of law, rule, or contract." The two elements common to both these definitions are: (1) the presence of broken law, and (2) punishment. In simplest terms penalty is punishment.

Where does the Scripture teach that Christ paid the penalty for the sins of men? Let us start with Galatians 3:10 and 13:

> For as many as are of the works of the Law are under a curse; for it is written, "Cursed is everyone who does not abide by all things written in the book of the law, to perform them." …Christ redeemed us from the curse of the Law, having become a curse for us—for it is written, "Cursed is everyone who hangs on a tree."

Here Paul says first that the curse of the law of God rests on those who break the law. The curse here is the penalty for sin. Paul's second point is that Christ bore that curse for us. Therefore, Christ bore the penalty of our sin (whomever "us" and "our" may represent). In commenting on Galatians 3:13, Bishop Lightfoot says: "The victim is regarded as bearing the sins of those for whom atonement is made. The curse is transferred from them to it." Sin and punishment (or penalty) go hand-in-hand here. But it is not we who suffer the penalty, it is Christ on our behalf.

Let us also look at 2 Corinthians 5:21: "He [God] made him [Christ] who knew no sin to be sin on our behalf, that we might become the righteousness of God in him." Here Paul says that Christ became *sin* for us. Some scholars would translate this as *a sin offering on our behalf*, but most reject this understanding because the word sin occurs twice in rapid succession. In the one case, when the text speaks of Christ as one "who knew no sin," sin offering cannot be the meaning. In some sense, then, Christ became sin.

As far as the grammar is concerned, Paul may mean one of two things. He may be telling us that Jesus became sinful and as a consequence we become godly. That would be grammatically possible, but in the light of all else in the New Testament, we know that

Paul would never mean that.

No doubt the contrast is not intended to describe moral states, but legal ones: Jesus bore our punishment; we receive his reward. In fact, this is the understanding of most Evangelical commentators except those who adopt the meaning sin offering. Here again sin and punishment go hand in hand. Christ bore our punishment, and we receive his right-standing with God. This verse does not tell us about two new moral conditions that he and we experience, but it describes our standing before the law of God. He was condemned so that we could be justified or declared right with God.

There is a second teaching of Scripture, closely related, that also demands that Christ died only for those who are finally saved. The Scripture teaches that Christ was the substitute for those for whom he died, dying in their room or place or stead. If one person dies in the stead of another, then that second person cannot die.

Let me illustrate. Suppose Bill Jones appears to be drowning and Joe Smith jumps into the lake to save him. Here are some possible results: (1) Both manage to save themselves. (2) Both drown. (3) Joe saves himself and Bill. (4) Joe saves Bill but drowns in the process.

Only one of these cases illustrates substitution. Which is it? It is the last one, the one in which Joe Smith dies in the place of Bill Jones. Does the Bible teach that Christ *substituted* for sinners?

Consider the following points. First, the idea of bearing a penalty for another implies substitution when the price paid is a person. If Christ bore my penalty and as a consequence I go free, then Christ has substituted himself for me. You can see that easily in the two passages we looked at previously. In the first case, Galatians 3:10 and 13, the curse should have fallen on *us*, but it fell on Christ. That is substitution. In the second passage, 2 Corinthians 5:21, Christ took my guilt and I received his righteousness. That, too, is substitution.

Substitution is also taught by Jesus as he speaks in John 10:11–15:

> I am the good shepherd; the good shepherd lays down his life for the sheep. He who is a hireling, and not a shepherd, who

is not the owner of the sheep, beholds the wolf coming, and leaves the sheep, and flees, and the wolf snatches them, and scatters them. He flees because he is a hireling, and is not concerned about the sheep. I am the good shepherd; and I know my own, and my own know me, even as my Father knows me and I know the Father; and I lay down my life for the sheep.

This is a part of a longer extended figure that the Lord Jesus gave us on himself as the Good Shepherd. Substitution is clearly in view in this discourse. When the hired hand (*hireling* is too strong) sees that he will have to suffer and perhaps die to spare the sheep suffering and death, he flees. He will not substitute his own life for the life of the sheep. But the Good Shepherd will (and in the application does).

This passage teaches particular redemption in another way as well. The Good Shepherd dies for his own sheep. That is clear in two ways: First, the parable is about sheep drawn from a larger group in one or more sheepfolds (John 10:1–4,16). Second, the one who dies is "the *owner* of the sheep" (John 10:12). This argument is not conclusive by itself, but in connection with substitution it bears out the particular nature of Christ's death.

We find the fact of substitution in Romans 3:24–26:

[Believers are] justified as a gift by His grace through the redemption which is in Christ Jesus; whom God displayed publicly as a propitiation by His blood through faith. This was to demonstrate His righteousness, because in the forbearance of God He passed over the sins previously committed; for the demonstration, I say, of His righteousness at the present time, that He might be just and the justifier of the one who has faith in Jesus.

Here Paul shows how Christ took the wrath of God in the place of men. Look first at the word *propitiation*. A propitiation is an appeasement, something that turns away the wrath of another. So Christ's death turned away God's wrath. But how did it do that? By having the wrath that belonged to us fall on him.

We know this because we are in the legal (forensic) realm here, according to Paul. Propitiation showed God's justice. But how does God show his justice in dealing with sin? By punishing it. By punishing Christ, God showed himself to be *just* and also opened a way to *justify* sinners (Romans 3:26). If what Christ did at the cross enables God to save men *justly*, then we are in the realm of law and penalty. Here again, penalty and substitution meet. And if Christ has substituted himself for me, then justice demands that I go free. Substitution is meaningful only where one dies and the other lives because of his death.

Let us look at one last verse that teaches substitution. Matthew 20:28 says "The Son of Man did not come to be served, but to serve, and to give His life a ransom for many." This brief verse indicates substitution in two ways. First, the little phrase, "for many," contains the Greek preposition, *anti*, that means "in the place of" or "in the stead of." The standard New Testament Greek lexicon says it is used "in order to indicate that one person or thing is, or is to be, replaced by another."[2] So Jesus here predicts that he will substitute himself "for many."

Second, the idea of a ransom, when the ransom price is another human being, is clearly another case of substitution. If a slave is being held for ransom and another slave is handed over to effect his freedom, there is substitution. If a criminal had been sentenced to death and another man becomes his ransom, bringing about his freedom, that too is a case of substitution. In Matthew 20:28 and the parallel passage, Mark 10:45, Jesus sets himself forward as the substitute for sinners. And if he substitutes himself for sinners, they go free. He could, then, have died only for those actually saved.

What is the effect of thinking carefully on these two ideas of penalty and substitution in the New Testament in connection with the death of Christ? They lead us to see that Christ purchased his people, his particular people, out of the larger mass of mankind. Does the New Testament teach that truth anywhere? Yes, it does.

As far as the fact of a purchase having taken place, we may look at such texts as Acts 20:28 and 1 Corinthians 6:20, and indeed, all the places Christ is said to have redeemed us, for a redemption and a purchase are the same thing.

Was that purchase from the larger mass of mankind? Listen to the singers in Revelation 5:9: "And they sang a new song, saying 'Worthy art Thou to take the book, and to break its seals; for Thou wast slain, and didst purchase for God with Thy blood men from every tribe and tongue and people and nation'." The purchase was a purchase out of the various people groups of earth; it was not a purchase of all of them.

ANSWERING OBJECTIONS

Let me come finally to the chief objections to what I have written about the particularity of Christ's death. We do not know our own position until we know what can be said against it.

First in order, I think, is the feeling that something precious has been denied to those who reject Jesus Christ if Christ did not die for them. But when one asks, "What advantage does the death of Christ give to those who are lost?" there seems to be no biblical answer. Many Christians[3] can only reply that the death of Christ becomes for the Christ-rejecter a ground of condemnation. That, of course, is no advantage at all.

One group of Christians, the Arminians, have a better answer if it were taught in Scripture. They say that the death of Christ has restored to all men the ability, lost in the fall, to turn to Christ in faith. But the Scripture does not teach this. If it did, it would make the natural man a mere hypothesis. Let me explain what I mean.

In such texts as Romans 8:7 and 1 Corinthian 2:14 we are taught the inability of the natural man. In Romans Paul tells us that the carnal mind, which is the only mind the natural man has, "is hostile toward God; for it does not subject itself to the law of God, for it is not even able to do so." Paul here is not speaking about some hypothetical man who no longer exists. He is speaking of natural men as they existed in his day. He says of them that they do not subject themselves to God's law. He says further that they do not because they cannot. Their hostility at God is so great that they cannot respond to the command, "Believe in the Lord Jesus Christ" (Acts 16:31). They cannot respond positively when God now commands "all men everywhere to repent" (Acts 17:30).

We find the same thing in 1 Corinthians 2:14: "But a natural man does not accept the things of the Spirit of God; for they are foolishness to him, and he cannot understand them, because they are spiritually appraised." Is Paul thinking here of some hypothetical man who now has had ability to understand spiritual things restored to him? No, it is plain that he is speaking of natural men as they existed when he wrote. What does he say of such men? First, they do not accept the things of the Spirit of God. Second, such things are foolishness to them. Third, they cannot understand them.

Someone may respond by saying, "Of course a natural man cannot understand the deep things of God, but he can understand the gospel and be saved." But a glance at the context will show that that misses Paul's point. It is the gospel itself that is foolishness to the natural man:

> For the word of the cross is to those who are perishing foolishness…God was well-pleased through the foolishness of the message preached to save those who believe…But we preach Christ crucified, to Jews a stumbling block, and to Gentiles foolishness" (1 Corinthians 1:18,21,23).

The conclusion is clear: Christ's death has not restored to all men the ability to believe. A death for all men, if that were what the Scripture taught, would be no advantage to the lost; it would be a liability, adding to their guilt.

A second objection to particular redemption turns on the universal words used in connection with the death of Christ, words like *all* and *world*. I have dealt with these words at great length in my book, *A Price for a People, the Meaning of Christ's Death*.[4] Let me confine myself to a few remarks here.

To begin with, universal terms in every language with which I am familiar are almost always used with very wide limitations. We do not often notice this, simply because we have taken it for granted since we were children. In fact, you may be surprised at this, but you will easily see that it is so. I'll take my examples from Scripture. Here are verses that illustrate it from John 3: "Behold, (Jesus) is baptizing, and all are coming to him" (3:26). "(Jesus) bears witness; and no man receives his witness"(3:32)." He who has received his witness has set his seal to this, that God is true" (3:33).

Note the apparent contradiction in this account of Jesus' ministry. In verse 26, *all* receive his witness and come to him. In verse 32, *no man* does so. But verse 33 assumes that some do in fact receive his witness. What is going on here?

Even if you have read this account many times you have probably never noticed this. The reason is simple: You are fully used to reading universal terms in a limited way, and you do it without giving it a second thought. You understand that verse 26 means only that a large number were coming to Christ, not literally *all*. In verse 32 you again grasp the idea: Compared with the number of people who should have responded to Christ, *no man* means relatively few. Verse 33 confirms your understanding: Some did, in fact, receive the witness of Christ. It never occurred to you to read all and no man as if they were true, universal assertions. You assumed the limitations on them and read on, without noticing what you were doing. You do that *all the time* (meaning often!).

Another example comes from Acts 2:17 where the KJV reads, "I will pour out my Spirit on all flesh." Think about that: all flesh. The NASV has translated this *all mankind*, thus eliminating almost every kind of flesh there is, with one exception. That is quite a sweeping change, yet it is correct. The flesh of turkeys and giraffes is not in view; God pours out his Spirit on men.

But even with the NASV's correction, eliminating most flesh, the alert reader eliminates still more. Is it true that God pours out his Spirit on all men (and women) without exception? No. So *all flesh* turns out to mean *some men and women*. In addition it implies a large number from many tribes and nations.

One last example comes from 1 Timothy 6:10 where the KJV reads, "For the love of money is the root of all evil." Is this true? Can we trace every evil in the world up to love for money? To ask these questions is to answer them. The NASV translators made this read "all sorts of evil." Is that better? Not literally, but it is if we impose our knowledge of idiomatic English on it. The English phrase, all sorts of evil, means quite a few evils. Again, the universal term is greatly reduced in our minds without any reflection on what we are doing.

We treat the word *world* in the same way. William Hendriksen in his commentary on John 1:9 distinguishes six groups or entities called the world. His list is not exhaustive. But let us look at the texts where some difficulty is found.

If we have been raised to think world in John 3:16 means every person who ever lived, we will take it that way. But there are other possibilities. World here may signify both Jews and Gentiles. In the context, Jesus has talked to Nicodemus, a man who probably held firmly to the common view that God loved the Jews but not the Gentiles. John attacks this idea elsewhere in his Gospel.

Or perhaps John 3:16 means that God loves mankind in the mass, a mass that he created. If a man says, "I love Englishmen," no one understands him to mean each and every Englishman, but Englishmen generally. Alternatively, B.B. Warfield held that the word world is used qualitatively here, not quantitatively. That would mean that God loved that which was at enmity with himself—another common use of world—however many actual people he might include.

1 John 2:2 reads: "He himself is the propitiation for our sins, and not for ours only but also for those of the whole world." Again there are several possibilities. John, being a Jew, might mean "not only for the sins of those of us who are Jewish but for Gentiles as well." It seems to me more likely, however, that he means to assert that there is no other propitiation. Anyone who will be saved—

however many or few—will be saved by that propitiation and no other. Still others think he may mean "He is the propitiation for the sins of those of us who believe and for the sins of all who will ever believe."

In the case of controversial passages, how we understand universal terms depends very much on how those who taught us understood them. Had you been taught that "God so loved the world" means that God loved both Jews and Gentiles, that is how you would understand it.

What does that prove? Prove may be too strong a word, but it strongly suggests that we must get our doctrine of the atonement from the words that describe it in Scripture and not from the universal terms that describe those who benefit from it.[5]

Words like redemption, reconciliation and propitiation, when applied to the death of Christ, show that his death was for his people and not for every person who ever lived. Does that seem threatening? It need not. What we all must remember is that everyone who puts his trust in Jesus Christ as Lord and Saviour will be saved. No one will ever believe only to find that there is no atonement for him or her.

The death of Christ is as broad as the category of believers. Beyond that it would do no good anyway. If Christ died for those who will never believe, his death would not help them in any fashion. It would only add to their condemnation. But Christ died for all who would ever believe. They, and no others, receive the benefit of the death he died for them.

5

MISUNDERSTANDINGS OF GRACE

I have sometimes wished we did not use the word grace. Is not that heresy? Consider for a moment what I mean.

We desperately need the content of the word *grace*, of course. The word stands for an idea that we cannot live without. I have no quarrel with that. But the word *grace* creates a problem for us. The problem is this: The use to which Christians put the word *grace* is not the use the word has in daily English. Our everyday English use of *grace* suggests a human virtue or quality of attractiveness. That leads to constant misunderstanding. For most believers, I think, grace is a rather hazy idea. That will be true even for those who have learned the little acrostic:

God's
Riches
At
Christ's
Expense

This essay first appeared in *Reformation & Revival Journal*, 3, No. 1 (Winter 1994), 33–44.

The acrostic tells us what grace gives us, but not what grace is. Now someone may say, quite rightly, that we have lots of theological words of which this is true. They are used in everyday English in a somewhat different way than they are used in the Bible and in our theological systems. Why then single out the word *grace*?

The answer is this: In many of those cases there is no plain synonym that one might use for the biblical or theological idea. We do not have that problem with *grace*. A clear and easy synonym for *grace* is *favour*. Simply put, God's grace is God's favour. When Paul, for example, describes himself as called by God's grace in Galatians 1:15, he means that it was by God's favour that he was called. It was a favour from God that Paul became both a Christian and an apostle.

Let us bring this closer home. If you have been saved by God's grace, then you have been saved by his favour. Salvation is yours because he favoured you. The gift of salvation is one of his favours to you. This is what the Bible means when it speaks of salvation by grace. It means that you and I and all other believers are saved because God favoured us over others. We have often heard that God has no favourites, but that is not true. He has millions of favourites, and the phrase "God has no favourites" would never have arisen if our English translators had given us the word *favour* where they have substituted the word *grace*. It is important to add, however, that God does not practice favouritism, a word that carries the idea of injustice with it in English usage. God is just. God gives every man and woman what that person deserves, or God treats him better than he deserves.

This chapter, however, is not intended to be a comment on the quality of our English translations of the Bible. I am sure that whatever faults they may have, I could not have done as well. My point is quite different. It is this: There are many misunderstandings of the idea contained in the word *grace*, and some of them can be traced to our unfamiliarity with the way the word is used in Scripture.

A THEOLOGICAL MISUNDERSTANDING

Let us start with a theological misunderstanding. This misconception is a bit difficult to explain, but widespread. It treats grace as a kind of substance that God pours into us. This may inspire the prayer, "Lord, give me your grace." That prayer should mean, "Lord, give me your favour," or perhaps, "Lord, show me your favour." In actual practice, however, the person praying the prayer may think of himself as lacking some spiritual substance within that makes him ineffectual in his Christian life. If he just had more of this stuff called "grace," he could do a much better job.

What is missing in this understanding? The missing element is the fact that grace or favour is not primarily something that is passed over to us from God. Grace is an attitude in God himself, an attitude of favour that reassures and strengthens the Christian. To paraphrase Romans 8:31: "If God favours us, who can be against us?"

Some theologians have traced this misconception of grace to the influence of the Latin word *gratia*, which began by meaning "favour" but, which, over time, came to convey the idea of a spiritual power that makes for right living. We can illustrate this change in the way the Roman Catholic Church has understood the virgin Mary. The kjv refers to her as "full of grace" (Luke 1:28). At first this meant "highly favoured" (niv). But in the course of centuries Mary came to be looked on as a repository or storehouse of spiritual power. She had "graces" that she could distribute to others. What at first was a description of God's attitude toward Mary became a description of Mary's qualities as a mediator between God and man. Of course Protestants never adopted this view of Mary, but many have come to look upon grace, not as an attitude of God but as a spiritual substance or power that he gives.

PRACTICAL MISUNDERSTANDINGS

However, in this chapter, I am interested in what we might call practical misunderstandings of grace and discuss two: (1) the misunderstanding that causes men to presume on God's favour or grace, and (2) the misunderstanding that causes men to fear or to despair of God's favour or grace.

Let us begin with the misunderstanding that leads men to presume on God's favour. Men misunderstand God's favour or grace when they think of it as unconnected with good works. Through the years, there have been men and women who have claimed to know God's saving favour and who have thought that salvation had nothing to do with good works. In the second century, a religion arose that is called Gnosticism, one branch of which claimed to be Christian. Some Gnostics treated morality very lightly. They reasoned that God will destroy this mortal body we live in, and what we had done with it would prove to be a matter of indifference to him.

Ideas of this kind were already afloat when John wrote his first epistle. He may have had this attitude in mind when he wrote, "If we claim to have fellowship with Him yet walk in the darkness, we lie and do not live by the truth" (1 John 1:6). People who held this view would profess to be "without sin" (1 John 1:8). Against such people John wrote, "The man who says, 'I know Him,' but does not do what He commands is a liar, and the truth is not in him" (1 John 2:4).

Many today seem to think that grace is unconnected with good works. A man once said from my pulpit, "My religion has nothing to do with good works." At the time I took him to mean that his justification did not depend on good works. If that is what he meant he certainly was right, as I hope to show shortly. Later, however, I saw reason to think that he meant exactly what he said, though I hope I misjudged him.

The doctrine of the security of the believer is sometimes preached in a way that leaves a godly life as an option for the Christian. It is looked upon as a desirable option, to be sure, but an option nevertheless. No doubt many pastors who hold this idea do so to protect the freeness of justification. Many of them also are zealous to see their people become more holy, and they preach with that in mind.

But the effect of such preaching is often to harden people in their sins. Pulpits where this misunderstanding exists never ring with the words, "Examine yourselves to see whether you are in the faith" (2 Corinthians 13:5). They do not often sound the note of Peter, "Therefore, my brothers, be all the more eager to make your calling and election sure" (2 Peter 1:10). If a godly life does not necessarily go hand-in-hand with God's salvation by grace, these texts are robbed of their force. After giving a long list of virtues that the Christian must eagerly pursue, Peter says, "Make your calling and election sure. For if you do these things, you will never fall, and you will receive a rich welcome into the eternal kingdom of our Lord and Saviour Jesus Christ" (2 Peter 1:10b–11).

The man who believes he has received the grace of God and yet does not pursue godliness deceives himself. He is not a characteristically carnal Christian; he is lost. His profession of faith is mere presumption.

Some preachers do not grasp this fact. I know this well, since I was once one of them. They are ready to reassure such a fellow that he need not have "a rich welcome" into God's kingdom; he may have a poor welcome, a welcome in which he will lose his rewards but gain his soul. To bolster this view they may cite Paul's words in 1 Corinthians 3:14–15: "If what he has built survives, he will receive his reward. If it is burned up, he will suffer loss; he himself will be saved, but only as one escaping through the flames." Clearly these verses picture some men losing rewards and making it to heaven. Oddly enough, however, these verses do not apply to the man who professes to have received the grace of God and yet lives an ungodly life. In a marvellous bit of irony, they apply to the preacher or teacher who reassures such a man that he is a Christian!

The passage in 1 Corinthians is not about any and every work. It is about one thing, the quality of our teaching. Paul wrote these words of those who sought to build up the church of Jesus Christ. Jesus Christ, he said, is the foundation of the church (1 Corinthians 3:11). Those who preach and teach are adding others to this foundation. As teachers they must be careful that they are adding true converts to the church. If they are careless in this matter, their work (their converts) will be destroyed, though they themselves will be saved.[1]

Once more, those who think that the grace of God is unconnected with good works are deceived. Further than that, they may be presuming on the grace or favour of God. If their lives are characterized by ungodliness, they are lost. They have misunderstood the grace of God.

Let us come finally to the other misunderstanding of the grace of God, the misconception that leads men to fear or despair of God's grace. Men misunderstand God's favour or grace when they think of it as dependent upon good works.

"Now wait a minute," someone may object. "Have you not just told us that grace depends on good works? Are you reversing fields?"

No, I am not reversing fields. Grace does not depend on good works in any way. What I have insisted on is this: Good works always accompany saving grace. But that does not tell us which depends on which. Grace does not depend on good works, but good works depend on grace.

Put another way, salvation is not by works, but works are by salvation. Or again, grace does not wait for works, but works come from grace. I repeat: Men misunderstand God's favour or grace when they think of it as dependent upon good works. Good works arise from grace, not the other way around.

The view that God's favour toward us depends on our works (or lack of works) takes various forms. Here are a two:[2]

1) *Christians misunderstand God's grace when they "live with a vague sense of God's disapproval."*
The operative words here are "a vague sense." If we know we have sinned a specific sin we must confess and, God being our helper, determine to forsake it. But a vague sense of God's disapproval probably arises from not understanding grace.

The truth is: God does not withdraw his favour because we sin. That, of course, does not mean that he approves of sin. Not at all! It simply means that he knew all about your sin and took it into consideration before he ever extended his grace or favour to you. To live with a sense that the Lord disapproves of you is to misunderstand grace. God receives you as he receives his Son. He receives you in Christ. This is true of every believer. To be sure, believers vary, but God's acceptance of believers does not vary. His favour rests on each of them all the time.

Someone may ask, however, "If that were true, he would not punish us, would he? Does punishment not show that we are no longer in his favour?" If we understand the word *punishment* properly, we will see the fallacy in this argument.

God has punished all the Christian's sins in Christ. There is no punishment left for us to suffer. All has been borne by Jesus. Notice this, however: here I am using *punishment* in its primary meaning, "A penalty imposed for violating law." None of this falls on the believer; all of it fell on Christ.

God does discipline his children. Sometimes his discipline is painful. We may also call that punishment. What we must not do is think of it as God no longer favouring us. Just the opposite is the case! " 'The Lord disciplines those he loves, and he punishes everyone he accepts as a son.' Endure hardship as discipline; God is treating you as sons" (Hebrews 12:6–7). See the argument? God's discipline is an evidence of God's love!

2) *Christians misunderstand God's grace when they "feel sheepish bringing their needs before the Lord when they have just failed him."*
Here is a common problem that I suppose none of us escapes. We need to pray for something, and we have just failed the Lord badly. Better postpone that prayer!

Do our failures make it less likely that the Lord will hear our prayers? Perhaps, if we are trying to hide our failure or sin from God. In that case, we may need to be disciplined by having the heavens seem as brass. Even then, however, it only seems so. The Lord is as attentive to prayer after sin and failure as he is to any other prayer. He does with that prayer what he does with every prayer offered by a believer: He answers it as seems best to him.

GRACE AND THE FORGIVENESS OF SIN

Why then do we have the impulse to avoid praying after sin? This gets to the heart of the issue. We feel that a certain amount of suffering and remorse must take place to restore us to God's favour or grace. It just does not seem right that he simply forgives our sin! It does not seem right to us; it does seem right to him.

This raises a larger question too. When does God forgive our sin? Did he forgive the sin of all his people when Christ died for that sin? Does he forgive all our sin, past, present and future, when we first come to Christ? Does he forgive our sin when we commit it? Or does forgiveness wait on our confession of sin? Which is it? This is a hard question, but I want to give you my judgment.

It seems clear to me that God forgives our sins as we commit them. Of course he forgave all our past sins when we came to Christ. That much seems beyond controversy.[3] Beyond that, however, the question becomes more difficult. Let me show you why I believe as I do, and then, let us look at the difficulties connected with my position.

It seems to me clear that justification, which includes the forgiveness of sins, is a present possession of believers. It is possible to think of justification as future only, something God will do for us on the judgment day. But that does not seem to me to agree with Scripture. We will, of course, be justified at the judgment, but justification is also a present possession of Christians.

Yet if we had even one sin unforgiven, we would not be justified; we would be condemned before God.

The only way to have all our sins forgiven at any given moment is for God to forgive them as we commit them. This would be true if sin consisted only of outward acts that we shortly confessed. There would still be a time lapse in which we were not justified, not forgiven. The upshot would be that we would be justified part of each day and condemned part of each day.

But the problem is more serious than that. Sin extends beyond the outward acts that are obviously sinful. It is a heart condition. It dwells especially in our motives and intentions. It is sometimes hidden from us as it propels us toward a wicked act. It may be working for days or weeks before it bears its outward fruit. The result? Given this fact, we would never be justified. We would always have sin that needed to be forgiven. Only if our sin is forgiven as we commit it can we be really just in the eyes of God.

That is my understanding. Let us look at the difficulties.

Two verses in the New Testament spring to mind immediately. The first is 1 John 1:9: "If we confess our sins, He is faithful and just and will forgive us our sins and purify us from all unrighteousness." This verse seems to say as plainly as possible that forgiveness awaits our confession. Is that not what it teaches? Not quite.

It teaches that those whose sins are forgiven are people who confess their sins. That is what characterizes those who are forgiven. If a man is not in the habit of confessing his sins, he is a lost man; his sins are not forgiven. The verse does not, however, tell us when his sins are forgiven—whether when he commits them, or later.

This point seems to me to be immensely important. Every one of my sins is forgiven or I am lost; but, whatever my intention, I will never confess all my sins in this life. Yet I remain justified. The Lord does not impute my sin to me. As Paul said, quoting Psalm 32: "Blessed are they whose transgressions are forgiven, whose sins are covered. Blessed is the man whose sin the Lord will never count against him" (Romans 4:7–8).

Does this seem to be too good to be true? It is the teaching of God's Word. It is for every believer. It applies to you.

Someone may object, however, that the Lord Jesus has told us in the Lord's Prayer to pray that our sins will be forgiven. Does that not imply that God does not forgive us until we ask him? No, it does not. You can see the truth of this if you compare the request for forgiveness with the other requests. When we pray for God's kingdom to come, we are praying for a future event. When we ask for his will to be done on earth as it is in heaven, that is, perfectly, we are again looking to the future. When we ask for our daily bread, we mean for the day or days in front of us. The prayer for forgiveness, then, may be a prayer for the pardon of our future sins. And that, I think, is what it is.

Let us consider one further objection. Someone may say, "If it is certain that God forgives our sins when we commit them, why pray about it at all? Why ask God to do what he is certain to do anyway?" The answer is this: God delights to be asked to do things he has already made up his mind to do. The Lord's Prayer bears witness to this fact throughout. Review its requests once more. What do you find? You find that the prayer is largely about things God is sure to do. His kingdom will come, for example. It is not in doubt at all.

Why ask God to do such things? What better prayer could a Christian pray? It amounts to "Your will be done!" It is like cheering our team on to victory. If eternal wisdom has decided to do something, a wise child will say, "Go for it, Lord!" And a wise child will say that about the forgiveness of his own future sins. Knowing his sins are forgiven, he will not hesitate to bring his needs before God even when he has sinned.

Let us look back for a moment. We have seen how it is possible to misunderstand the word *grace*. We may think of grace in salvation as a kind of substance or energy poured into us by God; but, in this context the word itself means "God's favour."

Once we have grasped the meaning of the word, we may still have one of two misconceptions. We may think of grace, or God's favour, as unconnected with godly works, allowing us to live in sin; but those whose lives are characterized by sin are not Christians. They do not truly believe in Christ.

On the other hand, we may despair of God's grace and fear him if we think of grace as dependent on works. That too is both false and dangerous. God gives us his grace freely. He forgives believers' sins freely. All of their sins! No amount of works can make us right with God.

The truth lies between these two extremes. The sins of believers are forgiven. There is no need for servile fear when we come into God's presence, not even if we have just sinned. The man or woman, however, who refuses to confess his or her sin has another problem. Even that person's sin is forgiven, if his lack of confession is the exception and not the rule. Otherwise, he has a problem greater than a single unforgiven sin. If his life is not characterized by confession, he is not a Christian at all!

Grace means favour. Every believer has God's favour already; it is not something he somehow has to find. Yet by God's favour every Christian's life is a life of good works. They may not be remarkable works, either in the sight of the world or in the esteem of the Christian himself. That is not necessary at all!

Our Lord Jesus spoke of a cup of cold water given in his name. That does not sound like much, but the operative phrase is "in his name." What the Christian does he seeks to do for the glory of God and of Christ. That is what makes his works good in the sight of God.

A Christian is not a perfect man, or a man on the verge of perfection; but, take his average act and you will find a godly act, an act done to please his Lord. The Christian life, the life of grace or favour from God, is a life characterized by righteousness and marred by sin. If it is not that, it is not the Christian life.

6

REFORMATION:
A PIVOTAL ISSUE

The Protestant Reformation is rich in images connected with Martin Luther. Our mind's eye sees him nailing his *Ninety-Five Theses* to the door of The Church of All Saints in Wittenberg on October 31, 1517. These topics for debate among theologians kick off the controversy with Rome—inadvertently, to be sure. Again, in April 1521, we can imagine Luther before Emperor Charles who has ordered him to recant. Charles Krauth has called this moment "the greatest scene in modern European history." What will he do? Listen: "I cannot and I will not retract, for it is unsafe for a Christian to speak against conscience. Here I stand; I can do no other. May God help me! Amen!"

Speaking of images, who cannot see brother Martin throwing his inkwell at the devil? These images, whether quite accurate or not, are vividly before us in the early twenty-first century.

The heart of the Reformation does not lend itself so readily to imagery. Theological issues rarely do. Images usually capture

This essay first appeared in *Reformation & Revival Journal*, 1, No. 1 (Winter 1992), 29–37.

action rather than thought. Chief among the thoughts of Luther was the idea he captured in the title of his book *The Bondage of the Will*. To most of us neither his thought nor the title are familiar. They conjure up no image at all. We simply stand blankly before them.

The issue Luther grappled with in *The Bondage of the Will* can be turned into imagery by asking the question, "Just how dead is the dead sinner?" There he is; look at him. What can you expect of him? Can he move his arms or legs? Will he clean his plate? Will he sneeze? Just how dead is he? Look again. Is he, or is he not, a corpse? Luther's answer: yes, he is. But what exactly does this mean?

For Martin Luther the natural man was a spiritual corpse, wholly insensitive to the will of God. In practical terms that meant the natural man would never turn to God. He would have to be resurrected from his spiritual death to do that. Unlike many Evangelicals in our time, Luther was convinced that the sinner could do nothing to gain eternal life. Even the sinner's faith would have to be given to him.

This is what Luther meant by the bondage of the will. The natural man is a wicked man in all his parts. Since he is wicked, his will is wicked. His will, in other words, *is bound to what he is*. To imagine wicked man exercising his will to turn to a good God is to imagine what has never yet happened in all the world. It has not happened; it could not happen. No amount of time—not even billions of years could produce one wicked sinner that would turn to God or Christ. Man is dead spiritually. Really dead! And his will reflects that spiritual death. Let us compare Luther's understanding with that of some other figures in Christian history.

At the beginning of the fifth century, a man named Pelagius wrote on this subject. Pelagius held that Adam's fall in Eden set a bad example for all mankind. That example, he argued, has resulted in the awful amount of sin and ungodliness that we see around us. All men have followed Adam's example, but they need not have done so. Their "free will" could have been used to serve God. All men need to do is to decide to exercise their wills for godliness and they will find that their wills will operate as robustly for righteousness as they have often operated for sin. Basically man, though sinful for sure, has within himself the power to serve God if he makes a proper choice. Martin Luther was definitely not a Pelagian!

Actually, Pelagius did not convince many theologians. In part that was due to the opposition of a much more famous name in Christian history, Aurelius Augustine. Augustine held the same view that Martin Luther came to hold a millennium later. No denomination, large or small, seems to have officially adopted Pelagianism. But Pelagius made his mark in another way. He led a number of theologians over the centuries to adopt what has been called Semi-Pelagianism. These men did not agree with Pelagius, but they also thought that Augustine was a bit too strict. What they taught was this: Man was just about as sick with sin as Augustine thought, but not quite. Although he could not please God on his own, he did retain the power to turn to God for salvation. Man is very sick indeed, but not quite dead!

Luther saw the Roman Catholic church as corrupt in several ways, but especially in this: The church had slipped into Semi-Pelagianism. The church no longer followed the Scriptures in viewing the natural man as dead; they saw him as merely sick. Luther thought the difference between sickness and death to be an infinite difference!

Luther was not alone in his understanding of Scripture. Jan Hus, who had been martyred in the previous century, had held the same view. Hus, in turn, had been influenced by John Wycliffe, the man who has been called "the Morning Star of the Reformation." Among Luther's contemporaries, Ulrich Zwingli, John Calvin and, indeed, all the best-known names of the Reformation period shared his view of human nature. They were sure that anyone who read his Bible with an open mind would see that the natural man is an enemy of God who must be given a new heart in order to turn to God. His "free will" is a cipher as far as its power to turn to God is concerned. "We shall do battle," Luther writes to Erasmus, "against 'free will' for the grace of God."

These men were radicals! But were they "radically" right or

wrong? Can we think of having a reformation and a great new awakening in our time apart from the convictions of these Reformers? We must judge the answer to these questions by asking what the Scripture teaches.

Paul, in his letter to the Ephesians, plainly teaches that the natural man is "dead in trespasses and sins" (Ephesians 2:1) and that the cure for this is found only in resurrection. The Apostle says in the same letter:

> But God, being rich in mercy, because of His great love with which He loved us, even when we were dead in our transgressions, made us alive together with Christ (by grace you have been saved), and raised us up with him…(Ephesians 2:4–6a).

This radical change from death to life is a work of (new) creation, totally done by the Lord. As Paul says, "We are His workmanship, created in Christ Jesus for good works…"(Ephesians 2:10). Quite obviously, dead men do not exercise faith. *Dead men do not do anything!*

There, someone says, is exactly the problem. Luther read these statements about death as though man were a literal corpse. The dead men the Bible talks about do all kinds of things! The objector is right about man's activity, of course. The Bible's dead men are still very active. But what do they do? Listen to the Apostle again in the same chapter of Ephesians:

> You were dead in your trespasses and sins, in which you formerly walked according to the course of this world, according to the prince of the power of the air, of the spirit that is now working in the sons of disobedience. Among them we too all formerly lived in the lusts of our flesh, indulging the desires of the flesh and of the mind, and were by nature children of wrath, even as the rest." (Ephesians 2:1–3)

Paul describes the activity of dead men in these verses, and it is not a pretty picture. How do they walk (Ephesians 2:2)? In the way the world and Satan would have them to walk. In what sense do they live (Ephesians 2:3)? Their "life" is being swept along by lusts, the desires of the flesh and the thoughts of the unregenerate mind. Is there any room here for God? Not without new life.

Paul makes this same point in 1 Corinthians 2:14: "But a natural man does not accept the things of the Spirit of God; for they are foolishness to him, and he cannot understand them, because they are spiritually appraised." Why will a natural man not accept the things of the spirit? Because "they are foolishness to him, and he cannot understand them." Sane men do not risk their lives on foolishness that makes no sense to them. What is it that looks like folly to the natural man? At one time I would have answered, *the deep things of God*. We all know, I would have added, that natural men accept the gospel; that is clear enough. So it must be the deep things of God that natural men do not accept. In saying that, however, I would have abandoned Paul. Why? Because Paul has just taken great pains in chapter one to explain that it is the gospel that both Jews and Gentiles find to be foolishness! Listen to him as he repeatedly makes the same point:

> For the word of the cross is to those who are perishing *foolishness*... God was well-pleased through the *foolishness* of the message preached to save those who believe...we preach Christ crucified, to Jews a stumbling block, and to Gentiles *foolishness*, but to those who are the called, both Jews and Greeks, Christ the power of God and the wisdom of God (1 Corinthians 1:18,21,23–24, *italics mine*).

It is not the deep things of God that the natural man rejects; *it is Christ in the gospel!* Without Christ he will be lost forever, and, in his folly, he will have nothing to do with Christ.

Now I think I hear another objection that goes like this: "If a natural man cannot understand the gospel so as to embrace it, how can he be held accountable? That is not fair, is it?" In answering this question we come to the heart of the difference between

Luther and his opponents, both then and now.

In the New Testament, ignorance of the gospel is often a moral issue. Remember how the Lord described the Pharisees? He said of them, "Let them alone; they are blind guides of the blind. And if a blind man guides a blind man, both will fall into a pit" (Matthew 15:14). Let me tell you a curious thing about this verse. You may have read it a thousand times without ever feeling that the words of our Saviour are cruel or unjust. Why not? Because you sensed the reason he said what he did here. The Pharisees' problem was not with their minds. It was a moral problem, a problem with their hearts. If they had loved God they would not have been blind to the greatness of Christ. But they hated God, and their blindness was their judgment!

So it is with all natural men. Since the Fall, the natural man has hated God, and his hatred of God blinds him to the truth of the gospel. Blindness, spiritual death, these are his judgments. In the words of Paul: "The mind set on the flesh is hostile toward God; for it does not subject itself to the law of God, for it is not even able to do so; and those in the flesh cannot please God" (Romans 8:7–8). "The mind set on the flesh" is the only mind the natural man has, and with it he hates God! Hence, he "cannot please God"—not now, not ever!

What bearing does this truth have on the Reformation of the sixteenth century? Does it have any bearing on our efforts at reformation and our prayers for revival in this day? Why were Wycliffe, Hus, Luther and Calvin so clear and so adamant on this *particular* theological truth?

Every Christian who thinks of reformation and revival must always begin by thinking of how to give glory to God. Why should God revive his work if others get the glory?

Martin Luther and the other Protestant Reformers had been brought by sovereign grace to the knowledge of Christ. In Luther's case, he had struggled long and hard to make himself right with God—fasting, praying, wearing a hair shirt and pouring into the ears of his confessor the roll call of his sins. All was to no avail; all was worse than useless! But then he found peace! That raised the practical question: Who should get the glory for his new-found life? In the Roman Catholic church, generally speaking, Luther thought he saw the glory of salvation being divided between God and man, between the God of heaven and the idol "free will." Was his fear justified?

The apostle Paul shared Luther's fear that man would get some credit for that which is entirely from God. In the same first chapter of 1 Corinthians that we looked at previously, he shares this fear with his readers by saying: "For consider your calling, brethren, that there were not many wise according to the flesh, not many mighty, not many noble [called]; but God has chosen the foolish things of the world to shame the wise…that no man should boast before God" (1 Corinthians 1:26–29).

Paul was on the lookout for man's boasting so that he might cut it off before it even got started. How does he do this? By telling the Corinthians plainly that they were as foolish as others, but they are now saved because of God's choice. It was not their free will that brought them to Christ, but God himself. That is why he adds, "But by his doing you are in Christ Jesus" (1 Corinthians 1:30). It is not the sinner's doing, it is God's. Why did God arrange it that way? "That, just as it is written, 'Let him who boasts, boast in the Lord'"(1 Corinthians 1:31).

Today, again, men and women who belong to the Lord are longing to see God revive his work. Perhaps God asks such people, however, "Who will get the glory if I answer your cry?" Every true believer in Jesus Christ will answer that question with a resounding, "To you, O Lord, be the glory forever and forever!" Yes, every believer will say that and mean it. A new heart, a new creation from God, could not answer in any other way.

Not every believer, though, will give that answer with full understanding of the teaching of Scripture. The answer I have given above comes instinctively to the minds and lips of the redeemed when they are not thinking argumentatively. But that is not the whole story. Many a man and woman has been redeemed by Christ and still finds himself defending the old idol "free will" when he is drawn into theological battle. In that way, God is robbed of his glory.

If we want revival and the moving of God's Spirit in the early twenty-first century, are we prepared to let our theology be formed by the Word of God? If we are, we will soon discover that man is not simply going down for the third time in the sea of life. Man is drowned in sin. He does not need a life preserver; he needs the power of almighty God to raise him up from the grave! Free will cannot help him; only free grace can resurrect the dead!

Martin Luther saw this clearly. Our help is only in the sovereign intervention of God. Men may go on resting on the thought that by their own will they may turn to God at any time, but if they think that, they are deceived. Let Luther have the last word on this:

> *The Diatribe* (a book defending "free will") constantly imagines a man who either can do what he is commanded, or at any rate knows that he cannot. But such a man is nowhere to be found. If there were such, then, in truth either the commanding of impossibilities would be absurd or the Spirit of Christ would be in vain. But the Scripture sets before us a man who is not only bound, wretched, captive, sick, and dead, but who, through the operation of Satan his lord, adds to his other miseries that of blindness, so that he believes himself to be free, happy, possessed of liberty and ability, whole, and alive…Hence, the work of Satan is to hold men so that they do not recognize their wretchedness, but presume that they can do everything that is stated."

If God does not deliver such men, if God does not revive his work, what hope is there? According to the Scripture there is none. It is God or nothing! *Soli Deo Gloria.*

SECTION II

Church life

7

THE EPISTLE TO THE HEBREWS AND WORSHIP

Every Christian knows what the book of Hebrews is, but what precisely is worship? In brief, worship is a response to greatness. Not just any response, of course! One man may meet greatness with defiance, another with craven fear. Neither of these qualifies as worship. We will not be far from the mark, however, if we call worship an appreciative response to greatness. A worshipper is a person who thinks he finds greatness in another and responds with admiration. A Christian worshipper finds that greatness in God and Christ. The Puritan Thomas Watson said that God calls us to be God-admirers,[1] and so he does.

Is there admiration of God in Hebrews? If the question means, "Does the writer admire his Maker?" the answer is clearly yes, as it would be for any Bible author. But in asking the question I mean two additional things. First, does he[2] supply us materials that will prompt our own admiration and worship? Second, does Hebrews speak directly about worship? In both cases, we will see that answer is yes.

This essay first appeared in *Reformation & Revival Journal*, 9, No.2 (Spring 2000), 115–129.

The word worship is not common in Hebrews (1:6; 11:21 only; both in Old Testament quotations; but compare 10:2). This should not surprise us. It is uncommon in all the letters of the New Testament. In part this is attributable to worship-words in Greek often referring to posture, to bowing and kneeling, things that interest narrators like Matthew and John more than others. (The New Testament is not necessarily indifferent to posture in worship. But its emphasis on inward attitudes naturally suggests different vocabulary.)

MATERIALS FOR WORSHIP IN HEBREWS

If worship is an appreciative response to greatness, the worship of God and Christ demands the display of their glory. We must see them to worship them. The Bible, of course, is full of this—not least the book of Hebrews. A major theme of Hebrews is to call his readers back to faith in Christ if they are wavering. To do this he lays out the case for the superiority of Christ to all other persons in the universe except God the Father and God the Spirit. More than that, he identifies the Son as God himself. The call to faith in such a person is immediately a call to worship as well. We will trace this case through the book.

Hebrews opens with three contrasts connected with revelation: "God, after He spoke long ago to the fathers in the prophets in many portions and many ways, in these last days has spoken to us in His Son" (Hebrews 1:1–2a). The first contrast concerns time. God spoke long ago and again in these last days. The second has to do with recipients. God spoke to the fathers but now speaks to us. The third contrasts the instruments he used. God spoke in the prophets but now in his Son.[3] This summary statement at the beginning of the book alerts us to three facts. We live in a better time, we are more privileged people and God's instrument of revelation is incomparably greater than any other.[4] Hebrews develops all three of these ideas further, but what interest us is this incomparably greater instrument, the Son of God. We will look at him in this section as Son, Heir, King and Priest.

The phrase *Son of God* is used in various ways in the Bible when applied to the Messiah. Early use suggests that godly kings of David's line were God's adopted sons (2 Samuel 7:12–16; Psalm 2:7,12). Such kings typified the coming great King who, as we now know, would be God's Son in still richer ways. In the Gospels, this richness emerges. The angel who tells Mary of her coming Child calls him "the son of the Most High" whose "kingdom will have no end" (Luke 1:32–33). So far, this is Messianic language easily recognized by the godly in Israel. But he said more: "The Holy Spirit will come upon you, and the power of the Most High will overshadow you; and *for that reason* the holy offspring shall be called the Son of God" (Luke 1:35, *italics added*). Here the angel identifies the Lord Jesus in his humanity as God's Son. The product of God's activity in Mary, the human being produced will "*for that reason* be called the Son of God." John's Gospel takes a further step by giving us much of the material from which the doctrine of the Trinity comes (John 1:1–18). Here the Son of God displays a glory that belonged to him in eternity past. Later, the Son speaks to the Father in these words: "Father…glorify Thy Son…with the glory I had with Thee before the world was" (John 17:1,5). To be the Son of God is to be God himself.

Hebrews reflects this whole development. More than that, it reaches its high point almost immediately. Who is this Son? He is the one "through whom also He [God] made the worlds" (Hebrews 1:2b). He is the Creator himself, "the radiance of His [God's] glory and the exact representation of His nature" (Hebrews 1:3a). Nor is Hebrews done! The Son sustains the world by his providence. He "upholds all things by the word of His power" (Hebrews 1:3b). Only a man blinded by sin could not see materials here for the most exalted heights of worship! But we are blind, so Hebrews presses the deity of Christ on us. The Lord speaks of his angels as ministers, but "of the Son he says, "Thy throne, O God, is forever and ever" (Hebrews 1:8). In the words of the Father, the Son is *God*. One point of all of this is to lead us to intelligent worship.

The idea of Jesus Christ as "heir of all things" (Hebrews 1:2) is closely related. In his letter to the Romans, Paul tells us that God himself is heir of all things: "For from Him and through Him and *to Him* are all things," with the consequence, "To Him be the glory forever" (Romans 11:36, *italics added*). It is clear that Hebrews could have adopted these very words for the Son. To be Creator is to be Heir. These are God's prerogatives. We are inwardly compelled to admire him.

Hebrews also describes the Lord Jesus as King, a title that calls for subjection. Subjection, of course, does not imply worship as an appreciative response to greatness. There is such a thing as unwilling subjection, as there are such things as unrighteous kings. The rule of God's Son, however, invites our appreciation. God speaks of the eternity of his kingship (throne). He bases that eternity on the righteousness of the Son:

> Thy throne, O God, is forever and ever, and the righteous scepter is the scepter of His kingdom. Thou hast loved righteousness and hated lawlessness; therefore God, Thy God, hath anointed Thee with the oil of gladness above Thy companions (Hebrews 1:8–9).

This means that no one who subjects himself to the righteous King will have reason to complain of his rule. Beyond that, he has earned his kingship by sharing the human condition. "[W]e do see Him who has been made for a little while lower than the angels, namely, Jesus, because of the suffering of death crowned with glory and honour" (Hebrews 2:9). Why was he crowned? *Because of the suffering of death!* Hebrews develops this fact to show how this King acts as a father to his children:

> Since then the children share in flesh and blood, He Himself likewise also partook of the same, that through death He might render powerless him who had the power of death, that is the devil; and might deliver those who through fear of death were subject to slavery all their lives....Therefore He

had to be made like His brethren in all things… For since He Himself was tempted in that He has suffered, He is able to come to the aid of those who are tempted (Hebrews 2:14–15, 17–18).

Believers are the children he aids as a kingly father. Surely we will want to admire and adore him for this also.

Hebrews closely ties the kingship of the Son to his activity as Priest. Psalm 110:2 declared of David's greater Son, "The Lord will stretch forth Thy strong scepter from Zion, saying 'Rule in the midst of thine enemies'." The entire Psalm celebrates the Messianic kingship of the Lord Jesus. But verse 4 strikes another note: "Thou art a priest forever according to the order of Melchizedec." Priest and King! Hebrews develops this twofold description, especially in chapter 7.[5] He describes Melchizedec as follows: "For this Melchizedec, king of Salem, priest of the Most High God, who met Abraham as he was returning from the slaughter of the kings and blessed him, to whom also Abraham apportioned a tenth part of all the spoils, was first of all, by translation of his name, king of righteousness, and then also king of Salem, which is king of peace" (Hebrews 7:1–2). This passage teems with suggestions about the kingship of Christ.

If Salem is Jerusalem, the connection with a Davidic Messiah cannot be missed. Then, too, who can receive the titles of king of righteousness and king of peace more suitably than our Lord Jesus? But Hebrews has already established the kingship of Jesus and turns his attention to Christ as Priest. This occupies chapters 7 to 10 and gives us more materials for the worship of the Son of God.

Hebrews first sets before us a contrast with the former priests of Israel. Acting under the Mosaic Covenant, they failed to open the way into God's presence for God's people. Their failure was the failure of the Law that was abolished at the coming of Christ's Priesthood.[6]

For, on the one hand, there is a setting aside of a former commandment because of its weakness and uselessness (for the

Law made nothing perfect), and on the other hand there is a bringing in of a better hope, through which we draw near to God…[S]o much the more also Jesus has become the guarantee of a better covenant (Hebrews 7:18–19,22).

This better covenant rests on the activity of our Priest in several ways. It hangs on his perpetual life (Hebrews 7:23–25). It depends on his power to save forever (verse 25). It hinges upon his person, as well, especially his incomparable godly character (verses 26–27). All of these facts call us to look in wonder and admiration at the Son of God, to be God-admirers indeed. Millions have been made worshippers by the sight of Christ.

DESCRIPTIONS OF WORSHIP IN HEBREWS

Whereas chapters 8 to 10 continue to offer us materials for worship, they do so in large measure by referring to the outward performance connected with worship in the Old Testament. Thus far, we have treated worship only as an attitude, but attitudes express themselves in forms. The true Old Testament worshipper expressed his worship of God, in part, by approaching the Levitical priests to carry out their ministry on his behalf. The writer is interested in how these Old Testament activities point us toward completed redemption by the Lord Jesus. He cites the work of priests particularly, and he shows how that work anticipates the work of Christ.

The central act in the Old Testament system of priestly rites was the offering of sacrifice. Through Israel's history there were always large numbers of priests, all from the tribe of Levi. These facts led Hebrews to say that there would have been no room for Jesus as a priest under the Mosaic Covenant:

> Now if He were on earth, He would not be a priest at all, since there are those who offer gifts according to the Law; who serve a copy and shadow of the heavenly things; just as Moses was warned by God when he was about to erect the tabernacle; for, "See," He says, "that you make all things

according to the pattern which was shown you on the mountain" (Hebrews 8:4–5).

Despite this, the Lord Jesus is a priest, a high priest, because the tabernacle was meant to picture a greater reality, heaven itself or the presence of God:

> [W]e have [the Son for] a high priest, who has taken His seat at the right hand of the throne of the Majesty in the heavens, a minister in the sanctuary, and in the true tabernacle, which the Lord pitched, not man (Hebrews 8:1–2).

We may think of the Levitical system as a means to get into God's presence symbolically. The people were barred from that presence. They could come only near the entrance of the tabernacle. The priests themselves were barred from entering the tabernacle, except on rarest occasions (Luke 1:8–9). Only the high priest could enter the Most Holy place where the symbol of God's presence resided, and that only once a year when he brought blood for his own sins and the sins of the people (Hebrews 7:27).

If all this seems contrived to keep people and priests away from God, at least symbolically, it is no accident. It is meant to show us the effect of sin. On the other hand, the Lord Jesus goes right into the presence of the Father, called here the *Majesty in the heavens*. And if priests act for people, as they do, we believers find ourselves in the Father's presence as well. The Law could not do this for us, but the Lord Jesus has done it! No wonder we worship him.

There is a sense, of course, in which all men are already in God's presence because God is everywhere (omnipresent). In speaking of God's presence, then, we are not thinking primarily in terms of location but of relation. Let me illustrate. After Adam sinned, God "called to the man and said to him, 'Where are you?' " (Genesis 3:9). The text suggests that God was "over here" and Adam was "over there." Since God may have taken human form in seeking Adam, the suggestion is correct. But the real separation between

Adam and God that the text emphasizes is not local but moral. A friend once told me that "God never asks a question for his own information." God knew were Adam was, and he could have appeared "there" at Adam's side, making the question unnecessary. What would have been the effect of that? We would have lost the sense of intense moral separation that the question conveys. "Where are you?" reminds us that Adam and God were a million miles apart spiritually and morally.

We must still, however, try to understand what it means to now be in the Father's presence. Again Hebrews refers to the Old Testament rites and symbols to make this plain; again, this truth turns on the superiority of Christ to the Old Testament priests. In Hebrews 9 he describes the work of the priests and draws a conclusion from it:

> [T]he priests are continually entering the outer tabernacle, … the high priest enters, once a year, not without taking blood, which he offers for himself and for the sins of the people committed in ignorance. [Then Hebrews draws his conclusion:] The Holy Spirit is signifying this, that the way into the holy place has not yet been disclosed, while the outer tabernacle is still standing,[7] which is a symbol for the present time. Accordingly both gifts and sacrifices are offered which cannot make the worshipper perfect in conscience…(Hebrews 9:6–9).

The priests were busy about the tabernacle in keeping with God's instructions to them. But the very building they used, the tabernacle (and later the temple) showed that they were not the ultimate solution to our alienation from God. Their sacrifices showed the same thing. The whole Mosaic service could not "make the worshipper perfect in conscience" (verse 9). It could not give the sinner who was conscious of his sins the conviction that God wholeheartedly received him. It required a better priest, a better service and a better sacrifice to do that. That priest is Christ. His service is the service of the New Covenant. His sacrifice is himself.

[H]e entered the holy place once for all, having obtained eternal redemption. For if the blood of goats and bulls and the ashes of a heifer sprinkling those who have been defiled, sanctify for the cleansing of the flesh, how much more will the blood of Christ...cleanse your conscience from dead works to serve the living God? (Hebrews 9:12–14).

Christ has entered the real "holy place," heaven (Hebrews 9:24). He has not rushed out again, only to repeat the experience hundreds of times (Hebrews 9:25). God is pleased and satisfied with his work. What is the significance of this? His sacrifice has cleansed his people once and for all. No such cleansing came from the Mosaic ritual:

For the Law, since it has only a shadow of the good things to come and not the very form of things, can never by the same sacrifices year by year, which they offer continually, make perfect those who draw near. Otherwise, would they not have ceased to be offered, because the worshipers, having once been cleansed, would no longer have had consciousness of sins? But in those sacrifices there is a reminder of sins year by year (Hebrews 10:1–3).

The failure of the Mosaic ritual is spelled out here. It contained an annual reminder of sins rather than eliminating "the consciousness of sins." It could not relieve men and women of an evil conscience. The practical effect of this was devastating. The godly Jew bore a guilty conscience much of the time. Worse than that, there was no way to get fully beyond that experience. What, then, became of his prayers? He could never be sure they were heard. Did God find his voice offensive? He could not say.

But are things all that different among Christians? Are Christians free from nagging feelings of guilt? Are their consciences clear? Follow me closely here. The subject of conscience is tricky, but we will invite Paul to help us with it:

> For when the Gentiles who do not have the [Mosaic] Law do instinctively the things of the Law, these, not having the Law, are a law to themselves, in that they show the work of the Law written in their hearts, their conscience bearing witness, and their thoughts alternately accusing or defending them... (Romans 2:14–15).

Here Paul describes unconverted Gentiles.[8] They did not have the Mosaic Law, but they nevertheless had consciences attuned to some of Moses' chief commands. We may think of the laws against stealing and murder, for example. Since conscience acts as a judge of how we act, their consciences would cry, "Innocent!" or "Guilty!" just as a judge in a court of law does. Of course, over time, they could teach their consciences to speak against some things and not others (1 Corinthians 8:8–12). They could also squelch them almost completely (1 Timothy 4:1–2). The point here is this: While we live, we train our consciences. If we train them by Scripture they will become more comprehensive and more sensitive. The godly Jew experienced that, and so does the Christian. Both felt guilty when they defied their consciences. God planned it that way.

Hebrews tells us, however, that the blood of Christ, his sacrificial death, is sufficient to quiet the conscience. The blood of bulls and goats could not do that (Hebrews 10:4). But the death of Christ can.

Why, then, do Christians still feel guilty? There are two reasons. First, a conscience trained by the Word of God must feel guilt when it recognizes sin. Schemes for doing away with this role of conscience are misinformed at best, and ungodly at worst.

The second reason, however, is the one that interests us here. The conscience is not sufficiently trained when it only cries "Guilty!" We want it to do that; we need it to do that. But that is not enough. It must be trained to cry "Innocent!" as well. Normally it does so when we do something right, but that is not the whole story. The reason guilt plagues many Christians is that once they have repented (turned from their sin), they have not trained their consciences any further. One more step is needed.

We must train our consciences to run to the blood of Christ!

It is a training process, just as sharpening the conscience about sin is. Perhaps the problem comes because we have not recognized that conscience must be trained. We train it against sin, when we read the Word of God, but we may have never thought of what we are doing in those terms. The Bible usually trains the conscience without our realizing it. That is where the rub comes in. In keeping with our fallen condition, some of us sharpen it against ourselves as we read, and neglect teaching it to run to the comfort of the blood. Yet both are necessary for the Christian life.

In all of this I may seem to have wandered far from the subject of worship, but I have not. The point of this long excursion is to say that every Christian is welcome in God's presence and to show what that means. Negatively it means to escape the burdens that often plagued the Old Testament believer's conscience. Those burdens generated fear. Positively it means that the New Testament believer may be fully confident that his worship and prayer are acceptable to God.

Hebrews shows us how this works out in practice:

> Since therefore, brethren, we have confidence to enter the holy place by the blood of Jesus, by a new and living way which He inaugurated for us through the veil, that is, His flesh, and since we have a great high priest over the house of God, let us draw near with a sincere heart in full assurance of faith, having our hearts clean from an evil conscience... (Hebrews 10:19–22).

His argument runs like this. What Jesus has done in dying has opened the door to God so fully that we may have utter confidence in approaching him. Our forgiveness is complete, since our sacrifice is perfect (Hebrews 10:15–18). There are no barriers between the believer and God. Worship, praise, thanksgiving and prayer, all the things we address to God, are equally acceptable to him. Since that is the case, we can run to him at any time!

We must train our consciences, then, to look to Christ. If your conscience denounces you, it makes no difference, unless you are determined to cling to your sin. Otherwise, a guilty conscience must be washed in the blood, and the sooner the better! Such is the confidence God wants you to have in the death of his Son. "You have just sinned!" your conscience may say. "You have no right to expect God to hear your prayer!" The conscience that says that is only half-trained. Yes, you did just sin. That much is true. But you have a right to expect God to hear you anyway. It is not a right that is natively yours. Nor is it a right you have earned. Rather, it is a right purchased by the blood of Christ, and it is greater than all your sin! "Let us draw near with a sincere heart in full assurance of faith, having our hearts sprinkled from an evil conscience!"

CONCLUSIONS

At the outset we asked two questions. First, does Hebrews provide us with material for worship? Second, does he speak directly about worship as well? Let us see what we have found.

Hebrews exalts the Lord Jesus. He does so by setting him forth as God's Son, as Heir, as King and as Priest. In these things and in all else, Jesus is superior to all other persons except the Father and the Spirit. Hebrews makes these points to call forth our admiration of Jesus Christ. Such admiration is worship. If we enter into the spirit of Hebrews we become God-admirers.

In addition, Hebrews discusses worship. He uses the Old Testament ritual worship to show what Jesus did in taking us by the hand and leading us into the presence of God. We see the Old Testament priests in a tedious round of sacrifice that could not cleanse the consciences of the worshippers for long. Once a year we see the high priest, apparently barely welcome into the tabernacle chamber that contained the symbol of God. We are told that sin was the barrier between man and God; but, thank the Lord, there is more to the story. That "more" is Jesus Christ.

The Lord Jesus is the high priest of his people. As such he has offered a sacrifice, himself, that erases the barrier of sin for all those that trust in him. Believers, therefore, may freely offer prayers and praise without feelings of guilt. Such prayers go straight to the throne of God, just as if the believer himself were there. Not even a bad conscience can hinder them, as far as God is concerned. That is how completely the sacrifice of Jesus opens the way to the Father.

You can see, then, that along with showing us the Lord Jesus in his various offices, Hebrews caps his efforts to make us worshippers by reciting the effect of Jesus' death. Not only are we to be overwhelmed by the greatness of the person of Jesus Christ, but his work demands our admiration as well. Its bearing on us is breathtaking. It is unmitigated good news for sinners like ourselves.

8

THE BOOK OF REVELATION AND THE SUBJECT OF WORSHIP

In the previous chapter on worship in the book of Hebrews, I pointed to two different ways a Bible book may affect our worship. First, it may give us materials for worship. Hebrews does that by lengthy descriptions of the glories of Christ. That is helpful in worshipping the triune God. Second, a book may discuss worship. Hebrews does that by describing the Old Testament system of sacrificial worship.

When we come to Revelation we find much the same thing. The book shows us the persons of the Trinity, the very thing we need to admire and worship them. More than that, however, it shows us scenes of worship. Though often symbolic, these scenes (unlike those in Hebrews) are directly relevant to us New Covenant believers. Worship, then, is very much a part of the book of Revelation.

MATERIALS FOR WORSHIP IN REVELATION

Descriptions of the Trinity appear already in the introduction (Revelation 1:1–8). God is the one "who is and who was and who

This essay first appeared in *Reformation & Revival Journal*, 9, No. 3 (Summer 2000), 93–106.

is to come" (Revelation 1:4; see also verse 8), an echo of his eternity. The name is based on God's self-revelation when he was about to intervene in Israel's history (Exodus 3:14). In adding the words, "who is to come," John again shows God as active in history. There is no suggestion that God stands aloof from his world. His activity, however, is seen in the works of his agent, the Holy Spirit—he is alluded to in the phrase "the seven spirits who are before his throne"[1]—and in the works of a further agent,

> Jesus Christ, the faithful witness, the firstborn of the dead and the ruler of the kings of the earth. [He is the one] who loves us and freed us from our sins by his blood, and made us to be a kingdom, priests serving his God and Father... (Revelation 1:5–6).

This summary of the person and work of Christ is loaded with good things for the believer, things that prompt worship. He faithfully witnessed to this fallen world in leaving it by death. That was not his last word, however. He rose again and now has all authority in heaven and earth (Matthew 28:18). Not even the kings of the earth are excepted. He holds them in his hands. We are reminded that the New Testament commands us to honour the kings of the earth (Romans 13:7; 1 Peter 2:17). How much more worthy is he of our worship and praise!

Next, John turns from the bearing of the Lord Jesus' activity on the world generally to its effect on his people. Gripped by awe, he drops description and breaks out in adoration: "To him who loves us and freed us from our sins by his blood, and made us to be a kingdom, priests serving his God and Father, to him be glory and dominion forever and ever. Amen" (Revelation 1:5b–6). And he is not done! He calls both the world and Christ's people to a further glimpse of the glory of Jesus: "Look! He is coming with the clouds; every eye will see him, even those who pierced him; and on his account all the tribes of the earth will wail. So it is to be. Amen" (Revelation 1:7). O come, let us adore him! We must see God and

Christ to worship them, and here, in his introduction, John sets them before us.

We turn next to the first vision in the book. John opens with a description of his circumstances as he wrote (Revelation 1:9–10). He was an exile on Patmos when he heard behind him a loud voice, a voice like a trumpet, commissioning him to write to seven churches (verse 11). He turned to see who spoke:

> [O]n turning I saw seven golden lampstands and in the midst of the lampstands I saw one like the Son of Man, clothed with a long robe and with a golden sash across his chest. His head and his hair were white as white wool, white as snow; his eyes were like burnished brass, refined as in a furnace, and his voice was like the sound of many waters. In his right hand he held seven stars, and from his mouth came a sharp, two-edged sword, and his face was like the sun shining with full force (Revelation 1:12b–16).

What John sees is clothed in symbols. There is a striking figure "like the Son of Man." John is dazzled and frightened, and reacts accordingly:

> When I saw him, I fell at his feet as though dead. But he placed his right hand on me, saying, "Do not be afraid; I am the first and the last, and the living one. I was dead, and see, I am alive forever and ever; and I have the keys of Death and Hell. Now write what you have seen, what is, and what is to take place after this. As for the mystery of the seven stars that you saw in my right hand, and the seven golden lampstands: the seven stars are the angels of the seven churches, and the seven lampstands are the seven churches" (Revelation 1:17–20).

John sees Jesus, but not the Jesus of mere human weakness and frailty. This Jesus shares the endowments of the Ancient of Days of Daniel 7:9, yet he is distinct. He is "one like a son of man"

(Daniel 7:13, margin) who comes with the clouds of heaven. And he comes for judgment as we see from other references in Revelation to the sword that proceeds from his mouth (Revelation 2:12,16; 19:11–16,21). A fearful vision indeed! No wonder John fainted. What a blessed word comes to him: "Do not be afraid!" This may, in fact, be a key to the entire sight:

> "Fear not;" for your fears are groundless. You are affrighted at your own mercies. The thing you fear is the very thing that brings to you salvation….That was indeed a vision of matchless and overpowering glory. But with all this awful and impressive grandeur, it was only a presentation in a single view, of the grounds of confidence and joyful hope which flow from infinite power and wisdom and love. So that in these very things John had the brightest evidence of his own and the church's eternal security and triumph.[2]

What looks to be a call to collapse proves to be an occasion for worship!

The letters to the churches in chapters 2 and 3 give us materials for worship as well. As the Lord Jesus speaks there, we see his godly attributes. His knowledge encompasses everything about the churches (see "I know," Revelation 2:2,9,13,19; 3:1,8,15). We see his power in various ways. He holds the stars that represent the angels of the churches[3] in his hands (Revelation 2:1). He can remove the lampstands that represent the churches from their places (Revelation 2:5) along with other acts of judgment (Revelation 2:16,22–23; 3:3,9,16). And he has power and determination to reward his faithful followers (Revelation 2:7,11,17,26–28; 3:5,12,21). He is, in fact, "the one who searches mind and hearts, and [who] will give to each of you as your works deserve" (Revelation 2:23). In adopting this description of Yahweh from Jeremiah 17:10 and elsewhere (Psalm 7:9; Proverbs 24:12; Jeremiah 11:20), the Lord gathers up the themes of his own knowledge and power for judgment and reward in one striking word.

Skipping for the moment chapters 4 and 5, we come to the beginning of the record of the seven seals. Here we see Father and Son in the act of bringing judgment. We meet their agents in the form of four horses and riders (Revelation 6:1–8). The agents are the symbols of the powers that God and Christ hold to bring the sweep of their wrath across an unbelieving world. In quick succession they conquer men (verses 1–2), create social chaos (verses 3–4), produce famine (verse 5–6) and unleash further death-dealing forces on humanity (verses 7–8). This is magnificent power indeed, breathtaking and awe-inspiring! It reminds us of God's earlier judgment on Jerusalem where he speaks of "my four deadly acts of judgment, sword, famine, wild animals and pestilence, to cut off humans and animals from it" (Ezekiel 14:21).

But is it justice? The fifth seal gives a partial answer to that question:

> When he opened the fifth seal, I saw under the altar the souls of those who had been slaughtered for the word of God and for the testimony they had given; they cried out with a loud voice, "Sovereign Lord, holy and true, how long will it be before you judge and avenge our blood on the inhabitants of the earth?" (Revelation 6:9–10).

This glimpse of a different scene reminds us that the judge of all the earth will do right. His people have suffered at the hands of a godless world. They cry to him for relief. While his martyrs rest from their labors (Revelation 6:11), the sixth seal shows that righteous judgment rolls on. Earth and heaven join forces to display God's might (Revelation 6:12–14). Men of all ranks tremble:

> Then the kings of the earth and the magnates and the generals and the rich and the powerful, and everyone, slave and free, hid in the caves and among the rocks of the mountains, calling to the mountains and rocks, "Fall on us and hide us from the face of the one seated on the throne and from the

wrath of the Lamb; for the great day of their wrath has come, and who is able to stand? (Revelation 6:15–17).

Here is the recognition of grandeur that we would call *worship* if it came from men in appreciation of the God behind the spectacle. But it does not. It is left to us who believe to stop our mouths and bow our heads in wonder.

The judgments that fall in Revelation come in series. When the Lamb opens the seventh seal we find seven angels with seven trumpets (Revelation 8:1–6). The blasts of their trumpets bring further dire judgments (Revelation 8:7–9:21). Nor is that all. Seven angels with "seven golden bowls full of the wrath of God" appear (Revelation 15:7). They pour out their bowls (Revelation 16:1–20). So severe are they that mountains and islands run from them, and men pay tribute to their devastating effect by cursing the God who sends them (verse 21b).

Even this does not exhaust the subject of judgment in Revelation (see Revelation 17:1–18:24; 19:1–20:10 and the climactic judgment on men in 20:11–15). Each of these displays the glory of God and of the Lamb. Each prompts wonder and admiration and worship from the people of God. But it is time to turn to the scenes of worship.

DESCRIPTIONS OF WORSHIP IN REVELATION

If Revelation is a book of judgment—and it is—it is also a book rich in descriptions of worship. This is in keeping with the purpose of the book, to show that God is sovereign in what appears to be a chaotic world and to show that his people are safe.[4] As the light dawns on these truths, men and angels rejoice, extolling the glory of God.

The first extended description of worship falls in two parts in Revelation chapters 4 and 5. Chapter 4 shows us the throne of God in a scene reminiscent of Isaiah 6. Around the throne are twenty-four elders dressed in white and seated on their own thrones (Revelation 4:4). Also there are "four living creatures" with animal and (in one case) human features (Revelation 4:6–8). Neither the elders nor the creatures are explained to us, but their function is clear, to worship the creator God. He is the focus. The creatures continually celebrate the holiness of God in familiar words, "Holy, holy, holy, the Lord God the Almighty, who was and is and is to come" (Revelation 1:8; compare with Isaiah 6:3). In praising God's holiness they recognize both his purity and his distinction or separateness from his creation. This does not mean he has abandoned his world, but that his own being transcends it.

> John's readers lived in a world (as we do) where evil was rampant and apparently all-powerful. Goodness was weak and frustrated and ineffectual. But John's very first vision of heaven shows that these appearances are deceptive… Our God is good. And He is the *Lord God Almighty*. Real power is not with evil, but with God who is holy. Nor is this a passing phase. God is He who *was, and is, and is to come*… God's power and eternal being ensure that His holiness will triumph over all evil.[5]

The twenty-four elders join the celebration by ascribing worthiness[6] to God. "You are worthy, our Lord and God, to receive glory and honour and power, for you created all things, and by your will they existed and were created" (Revelatioin 4:11). As Creator, God deserves recognition and admiration. If this is seen to be true in heaven, we too must acknowledge it by our own appreciation and praise. We may adopt these very words as our own.

When we turn to chapter 5 the scene focuses in two senses on the right hand of God. There is something in God's right hand. More than that, there is someone at his right hand, one who shares the rule with him (see also Revelation 3:21).

> Then I saw in the right hand of the one seated on the throne a scroll written on the inside and on the back, sealed with seven seals; and I saw a mighty angel proclaiming with a loud voice, "Who is worthy to open the scroll and break its seals?" And no one in heaven or on earth or under the earth was able to open the scroll or to look into it. And I began to weep

bitterly because no one was found worthy to open the scroll or to look into it. Then one of the elders said to me, "Do not weep. See, the Lion of the tribe of Judah, the Root of David, has conquered, so that he can open the scroll and its seven seals" (Revelation 5:1–5).

Again we are faced with symbolism that is not explained. What precisely is the scroll with seven seals? Is it a deed? Is it a covenant, or some third or fourth thing? The commentators do not agree among themselves, but we need not be put off by this. The scene sets a Lamb before us, and the following chapters show him opening the seals and bringing history as we know it to its end by judgment and the introduction of a new heaven and a new earth. These central matters arise from his worthy work and will lead to "blessing and honour and glory and might" being ascribed to him and to God "forever and ever" (Revelation 5:13)!

A closer look at the Lamb shows us how his work could lead to such earth-shaking events. As Lion of the Tribe of Judah and Root of David (Revelation 5:5), he is the Messiah who came as conqueror to establish God's kingship in the earth. He is also, however, the Lamb who has been slaughtered. Already in Isaiah 53 Yahweh revealed that misunderstanding, oppression and death were the conditions of his conquest, but now that is behind him. The universe acknowledges his worthiness.

The lamb receives the worship of the heavenly attendants just as God had in chapter 4, but now the circle of worship expands, so that every creature in heaven and on earth and under the earth and in the sea worships "the One who is seated on the throne and the lamb" (Revelation 5:13).[7]

Why do men and creatures flock to this celebration? Because his slaughter was not in vain: By his death he has transformed humanity and history in preparation for the new heavens and earth. "[B]y your blood you ransomed for God saints from every tribe and language and people and nation; you have made them to be a kingdom and priests serving our God, and they will reign on the earth"

(Revelation 5:9–10). Here are the grounds of his worship. And here is its content: "Worthy is the Lamb that was slaughtered to receive power and wealth and wisdom and might and honour and glory and blessing" (Revelation 5:12)! May God give us the grace to join this song now and in eternity!

Revelation chapter 7 contains a third scene of worship (verses 9–17). In its early verses (verses 9–12) it reproduces something of the praise we have met in chapter 5. (The repetition emphasizes how appropriate it is to praise God and Christ for their mighty acts repeatedly.) Then John introduces a sight in which a heavenly being asks him a question:

> Then one of the elders addressed me, saying, "Who are these, robed in white, and where have they come from?" I said to him, "Sir, you are the one who knows." Then he said to me, "These are they who have come out of the great ordeal; they have washed their robes and made them white in the blood of the Lamb. For this reason they are before the throne of God, and worship him day and night within his temple" (Revelation 7:13–15a).

We are reminded by this description of the words of the psalmist: "Let the redeemed of the Lord say so, those he redeemed from trouble…" (Psalm 107:2). It is appropriate for all the creatures of the earth to praise the Lord, but none have more reason than those whose robes have been made white in the blood of the Lamb. But the elder is not done. He recites the further benefits of the redeemed, for which they praise their God. The language mixes figures with small glimpses of future reality. God will shelter them, secure them from hunger and thirst, and keep them from suffering any scorching heat (Revelation 7:15b–16). In other words, they will experience the blessings of Isaiah 49:10 and Psalm 23, "for the Lamb at the center of the throne will be their shepherd, and he will guide them to springs of the water of life" (Revelation 7:17). Their quality of life is summarized finally in another figure that reminds us of the divine intention of good for his people: "God will wipe every tear from their eyes" (Revelation 7:17b). Salvation from the penalty for sin will be followed by spiritual prosperity forever. But these promises belong to all believers; they are part of our *hope*. Here again is a call to us to worship as they worship.

The blowing of the seventh trumpet in chapter 11 brings us to another scene of worship celebrating the kingship of God through his agent, the Messiah. In Revelation 11:15 God and Messiah appear together in a way reminiscent of Psalm 2. There they contemplated the destruction of their future enemies. Here they are congratulated by loud voices from heaven for having finished their task. The scene is proleptic, anticipating the victory which will come to pass quickly. God's kingdom has come at last. He has exercised his great power in the midst of rebellion:

> The nations raged, but your wrath has come, and the time for judging the dead, for rewarding your servants, the prophets and saints and all who fear your name, both small and great, and for destroying those who destroy the earth (Revelation 11:18).

How soon would all this happen? Heaven seems to resound with the answer: "Then God's temple in heaven was opened, and the ark of his covenant was seen within his temple, and there were flashes of lightning, rumblings, peals of thunder, an earthquake, and heavy hail" (Revelation 11:19). Can the day be far off?

The theme of worship on the occasions of God's judgments appears through much of the rest of the book (Revelation 12:10–12; 15:3–4; 16:5–7; 19:1–4). It is unnecessary to discuss all of these, but chapter 12 deserves special attention. The chapter opens (verses 1–6) with a highly symbolic vision of the birth of the Messiah, our Lord Jesus, from the godly remnant of Israel under the figure of a woman.[8] The dragon, Satan, prepares to destroy him but is foiled by God's activity. Then follows an account of war in heaven in which Satan and his angels were cast down to earth (Revelation 12:7–9). This leads to worship by an unnamed voice from heaven:

Now have come the salvation and the power and the kingdom of our God and the authority of his Messiah, for the accuser of our comrades has been thrown down, who accuses them day and night before our God. But they have conquered him by the blood of the Lamb and by the word of their testimony, for they did not cling to life even in the face of death (Revelation 12:10–11).

Several things call for comment here. First, the note of successful judgment on the part of God is clearly sounded here. Whether we think of the book's bearing on men and women of the first century or our own century or the final century, we must remember the aptness of this theme. Though severity differs from age to age and place to place, the church is called to suffering for Christ in every age. In all her perils her comfort lies in the sovereignty and wisdom of God. That lay behind the word to John in Revelation 1:17–18, "Do not be afraid; I am the first and the last, and the living one. I was dead, and see, I am alive forever and ever; and I have the keys of Death and Hades." God is still in charge; Christ shares his throne. The hour may be dark, but our enemies will be defeated.

Second, the power that lies behind our enemies, Satan himself, is in the hands of God, to do with as he pleases. Third, "the blood of the Lamb and…the word of their testimony," leading even to martyrdom, is sufficient protection in the bleakest hour. His blood (his sacrificial death) covers the sins of his people while they remain loyal to him.

For all these reasons the worshipping voice from heaven calls us to join the chorus of appreciation, thanksgiving and praise to God.

The mood changes in the final two scenes of worship in Revelation (Revelation 19:5–8; 21:3–4). They celebrate the final union of God and his people. Let us look more closely at the first of these:

And from the throne came a voice saying, "Praise our God, all you his servants, and all who fear him, small and great." Then I heard what seemed to be the voice of a great multitude, like the sound of many waters and like the sound of mighty thunderpeals, crying out, "Hallelujah! For the Lord our God the Almighty reigns. Let us rejoice and exult and give him the glory, for the marriage of the Lamb has come, and his bride is ready; to her it has been granted to be clothed with fine linen, bright and pure"—for the fine linen is the righteous deeds of the saints (Revelation 19:5–8).

As important as judgment was and is, it is preliminary to the final phase of redemption. Judgment casts aside the unsuitable fish (Matthew 13:47–50) and blows away the chaff (Matthew 3:12; 13:30), but that is not the goal of history; God's union with his people is.

Heaven rejoices over this union, and so must we who are the bride at this wedding. The mark of a joyous wedding feast is the mutual admiration of bride and bridegroom. What God sees in us is what he has put in us, but what we see in him is what has been natively his forever, his love and compassion and mercy over his people. Are there greater themes to celebrate than these? O, come let us adore him!

SUMMING UP

The study of worship can never be an academic matter. It involves our lives at their deepest points, our relations to God. At the same time, we must see that a detached, academic view of the subject is inevitable if our hearts are not fixed on God. That is why prayer and praise (worship) go hand in hand. The apt response to a study like this is to cry out to God for a fuller measure of grace. If he grants that prayer, we will admire, worship and adore him. And if we are wise, we will let what we have found in this study of Revelation and worship inform our acts of praise and thanksgiving to our God.

9

UNITY AMONG CHRISTIANS AND SUBSCRIPTION TO CREEDS

The barriers to unity among Christians are formidable, and no one must imagine that solutions that arise from unaided human intellect will overcome them. The problems are spiritual. We are divided because of our sinfulness, and our divisions are one aspect of the loss of objectivity within a fallen race. Yet objectivity eludes us. I have it, of course; who could doubt it! But your inability to see beyond your hastily conceived, narrow convictions guarantees that our minds will never meet! We are doomed to division until a brighter day dawns forever. Why can you not see things my way? Who shall deliver us from this body of conceptual death?

As with other spiritual problems, however, the Scriptures demand our efforts. The fact that a problem arises from sinfulness is a call to attack it with fervour. Individually we must repent of our arrogance in not listening to our brothers and sisters in Christ with sympathy. But corporately…what can we do corporately? In this chapter, I discuss a single barrier to unity. What I say may be

This essay first appeared in *Reformation & Revival Journal*, 7, No. 4 (Fall 1998), 149–161.

summarized in two short sentences:

1) Our creeds and confessions are one immense barrier to unity.
2) There is no easy or obvious way to cross this divide.

If my first sentence sounds to you like an indictment against treasured historical and doctrinal landmarks, I simply remind you that one function of creeds is to exclude; no one should be surprised at this. If the second seems pessimistic, keep in mind that there can be no solution without a frank recognition of the problem created by the documents for which some among us are prepared to die.

Creedal unity has a long and honourable history. Beyond gathering for minor events such as ice cream socials and softball tournaments, whatever the church of Jesus Christ does is done on a doctrinal foundation. The absence of a written creed is no real exception. United effort means the presence of common convictions wherever men and women enter intelligently into labour for the Lord. This is nicely and authoritatively illustrated in the earliest church as seen in the book of Acts. We need not confine their "one mind" (Acts 2:46) to doctrine, to the exclusion of all else, to see that if they did not share the Apostles' doctrinal teaching they could not have joined as heartily in the fellowship, breaking of bread and prayer (Acts 2:42).

Nor is that all. Paul insists on doctrinal unity in reminding the Ephesians that "There is one body and one Spirit, just as also you were called in one hope of your calling; one Lord, one faith, one baptism, one God and Father of all who is over all and through all and in all" (Ephesians 4:4–6). Such teaching makes it impossible to think that any and every opinion may be called Christian and used as a basis for united effort.

It is sometimes thought that the Bible itself is a sufficient basis for unity. After all, any doctrine that can be called Christian must finally be traced to the written Word of God. Why not, then, simply rest upon the Scriptures? In recent years we have heard men and women respond to traditional categories like *Calvinist* and

Arminian with the assertion that they are *Biblicists*. What is wrong with that?

There is nothing wrong with the word *Biblicist* itself. But what does it mean? If it is the simple assertion, "I believe the Bible!" we may approve it, even applaud it, but we cannot help remembering the large number of cultists who say the same thing with the same eager enthusiasm. If it means more than "I believe the Bible!" then those who unite on it have some common understanding about what the Bible teaches. There is no middle ground here. A creedal basis of some greater or lesser degree of precision, written or understood, undergirds all common activity among Christians. A creed asserts, in the words of a booklet issued by the Free Reformed Churches of North America, that:

> We are united, not merely by a vague respect for Scripture, but by a deep-rooted commitment to a common understanding of its message. Our creeds are a declaration of the doctrines which we hold in common.[1]

Groups that have opposed writing down their common convictions have had them nevertheless. And they have held them tenaciously! Witness the so-called Plymouth Brethren and the Churches of Christ.

Whereas the points I have made above are widely accepted, it seems to me that most Christian groups have not given sufficient thought to the difficulties created by our creeds and confessions. There are, to be sure, exceptions to this judgment. At the departure of our Pilgrim forefathers for the New World, their pastor, John Robinson, made a speech described for us by Edward Winslow:

> We were now ere long to part asunder; and the Lord knoweth whether ever he [Robinson] should live to see our faces again. But whether the Lord had appointed it or not; he charged us, before God and his blessed angels, to follow him no further than he followed Christ: and if God should reveal anything to us by any other instrument of his, to be as ready to receive it,

as ever we were to receive any truth by his Ministry. For he was very confident the Lord had more truth and light yet to break forth out of his holy Word.

He took occasion also miserably to bewail the state and condition of the Reformed [i.e., Protestant] Churches, who were come to a period in religion; and would go no further than the Instruments of their Reformation. As, for example, the Lutherans: they could not be drawn to go beyond what Luther saw, for whatever part of God's will He had further imparted and revealed to Calvin, they will rather die than embrace it. And so also, saith he, you see the Calvinists. They stick where he left them, a misery much to be lamented.[2]

Although we recognize that Robinson was speaking of groups of Christians rather than written creeds *per se*, several things call for comment. First, Robinson himself, though an independent, was no doubt a Calvinist so that this is not a criticism from wholly outside the circle of those he seeks to correct. Second, he believes that there is yet more truth for Christians to discover in God's Word. Unless he thought this further truth would not contradict any tenet already held by Lutherans and Calvinists, a thing very unlikely in itself, he is implicitly calling for creedal corrections and additions. Third, he thinks he detects an unwillingness among his fellow Protestants to do such correcting and addition. Sadly, history bears out this judgment. Only the slightest changes have been made in most of the creedal forms that arose as a result of the Reformation.

Let me illustrate the difficulty with the words of Matthaeus Flacius, a sixteenth-century Lutheran:

Every understanding and exposition of Scripture is to be in agreement with the faith. Such [agreement], is, so to speak, the norm or limit of a sound faith, that we may not be thrust over the fence into the abyss by anything, either by a storm from without or by an attack from within (Romans 12:6). For everything that is said concerning Scripture, or on the basis of Scripture, must be in agreement with all that the catechism declares or that is taught by the articles of faith.[3]

Several things call for comment here. First is the demand for all interpretation of Scripture to agree either with the Lutheran catechism or with "the articles of faith," presumably, the *Augsburg Confession*. For someone standing outside the Lutheran tradition this seems to be a demand to give up *sola scriptura*. We need not deny the importance of Martin Luther and Philipp Melanchthon in the providential arrangements of God to see that they have no right to stand between ourselves and God's revelation in his Word.

What most of us must see, however, is that this situation is just as egregious if our tradition looks to John Calvin or John Wesley or to the authors of the *Thirty-Nine Articles* or the *Westminster Confession*. In each case we must allow Scripture to speak for itself. As Daniel P. Fuller has written in commenting on Flacius' statement above:

> This statement of Flacius shows how Luther's use of the analogy-of-faith principle had made church tradition, fixed in creeds and catechisms, the key for the interpretation of scripture. Even though this tradition was now of a Protestant rather than of a Roman Catholic variety, yet the barrier which it erected against letting biblical exegesis improve or correct that tradition was exceedingly hard to surmount.[4]

Christians of all persuasions must seek to take this seriously. What has developed in church history is the claim that Scripture alone is our standard, joined to the quiet and often unrecognized co-principle that our confessions are the traditions by which we must read God's Word.

We must also examine Flacius' reference to Romans 12:6. There Paul has written, "And since we have gifts that differ according to the grace given to us, let each exercise them accordingly: if prophecy, according to the proportion (*analogian*) of his faith."

Commentators are divided on the understanding of "the proportion [or analogy] of faith," but even if we take it as a standard to which all exegesis must conform, it is clear that it must be a standard that existed prior to Paul's writing of Romans. That does not mean that there could be no growth in it as more of the New Testament was written, but to suppose that it conforms exactly to one of the post-Reformation confessions strains credulity beyond reasonable limits. Again, on the assumption that a standard is in view, the most it may demand of us is to understand more obscure Scripture in the light of what is dearer and simpler. (This is, in fact, the way the phrase "the analogy of faith" has often been used in church history.)

Although the confessions have tended to control our under-standing of Scripture, something even less frequently recognized has added to our difficulty. At least until the present century, our conservative systematic theologies have tended to be expositions of the confessions even when that was not immediately apparent. The reason for this is not difficult to determine: The systematic theologian doing the writing was usually already bound to a con-fession by being a member or theologian of a confessional church. He could keep neither his credentials as a minister nor his post as a theological professor if he varied appreciably from the confession of his church.

This does not mean—and I do not want to be understood as saying—that such men compromised their convictions for the sake of their positions. I have no way of knowing their motives and, more than that, I am an admirer of the men in my theological tradition. It does mean, however, that they were producing theo-logical works that did very little to question confessional stances, however pure their motives may have been.

Now you will see immediately how all of this bears on unity among believers. Surely we must unite on truth, but as I wrote earlier, the confessions and creeds are a barrier between us. This is what we might have expected, but that is not all. The little impact that Lutherans have had on Calvinists, and vice versa, bears witness that some constraint has kept them from freely and openly working to eliminate their differences in the last 300 years. Creedal statements were intended to unite, but also to exclude, and they have succeeded on both fronts. Is there a single substantive area in which Lutherans have convinced their Calvinistic brothers? Has any change been made in the Lutheran confessions of the last 300 years that demonstrates the cordial embrace of any Calvinistic idea? Is it any consolation for those who long for unity among believers in Christ, that each side can say, "But we are right!"? Each side—and every other side that may reasonably be called Christian—has had the responsibility before God to strive for unity in a scriptural way. Can anyone doubt that the large measure of failure can be traced, humanly speaking, to strict subscription to creeds? On the other hand, it is with heavy heart that I admit that finding a solution to this problem is more difficult than simply describing it. I have shown earlier that the abandonment of creedal statements cannot be the cure-all. Too much is at stake.

What can we do? The central matter is that those who study the Scriptures must have liberty to follow them wherever they may lead. How can we obtain such liberty in a creedal world?

The possibilities, it seems to me, must lie somewhere along the following lines. None of these solutions will commend itself to everyone, but we need to consider them:

1) *A major simplification of our creeds.*
I have already alluded to the large number of confessions upheld by Lutherans. But we must not think of them as exceptional. A number of Calvinistic denominations subscribe to the Apostles' Creed, the Nicene Creed, the Athanasian Creed, the *Belgic Confession*, the *Heidelberg Catechism* and the Canons of Dort. Other groups subscribe to fewer creeds, but their confessions of faith are lengthy and detailed. Each group must seriously ask itself if all this detail is necessary.

2) *A looser subscription to creedal statements.*
Would anyone today defend the following subscription terms that the French churches adopted in 1620?

I N[ame]. N[ame]. do Swear and Protest before God, and this Holy Assembly that I do receive, approve and imbrace [sic] all the Doctrines taught and decided by the Synod of Dort, as perfectly agreeing with the Word of God, and the Confession of our Churches. I swear and Promise to persevere in the Profession of this Doctrine during my whole life, and to defend it with the utmost of my power, and that I will never, neither by Preaching nor Teaching in the Schools, nor by Writing depart from it.[5]

Certainly "loose" subscription is preferable to swearing never to change one's mind in one's "whole life"! The problem here, of course, is "How loose is loose?" If this looseness is defined in detail, the result is likely to be a slightly smaller confession to which all must strictly subscribe! Yet in the past, some groups have apparently found a way to do this. Let me cite one illustration, the Baptists of the Philadelphia Association, who subscribed to the *Philadelphia Confession* (a slight variant of the *1689* or *Second London Confession*). Each year this association issued a circular letter to all the churches. The following is taken from the letter of 1798, titled *Religious Worship and the Sabbath Day*:

[I]t is to be wished that all Christians were unanimous on this subject; but there is little hope of this being the case, till we drop all traditions and traditional modes of speech; for these things will cause many mistakes.

The compilers of our confession of faith were desirous to use the same language with other Christians, as far as was thought consistent with a good conscience; and it may be, on this subject, they conformed more than can be supported by the Holy Scriptures, or any arguments justly drawn from them...[W]e proceed to show that the fourth command was not moral, notwithstanding it is sometimes placed with moral commands...[6]

As suggested by his own words, the writer, David Jones, goes on to argue against the language of his confession, showing that in at least one important respect he was a loose subscriptionist.

3) *Encouragement for change within the confessions themselves.*

Perhaps our confessions of faith must include more than a general statement that all writings of uninspired men are bound to err. Perhaps in addition they must contain a statement to the effect that *this confession itself* falls under this general condemnation. And perhaps they must last of all include a statement of willingness to be reproved from Scripture that quite evidently expects to have that done. When the confessions of men genuinely challenge others to question them without fear of consequences, then we will have arrived at confessions that demand our respect in a new way. At least one solid gain would come from such an approach. Questions about the truth or falsity of statements in the confessions would now come from within the groups of adherents. Of those men who think they find a flaw in their confessions, who is better to raise questions: the man whose integrity now forces him to abandon them, when he agrees with most of what is written, or the man who stays within the group of adherents and keeps his reservations to himself? Can there be any doubt as to the answer to this question?

4) *To be creative let us invent something on the spur of the moment.*

It may be that a denomination, an association or even a local church could rate deviations from its standards as to the degree of departure it will tolerate. In this scenario each item in the confession would be awarded a score. A few basic matters would be awarded an "N" for non-negotiable. The rest would be rated from one to ten, ten representing the most important matters. If a member or deacon or elder compiled a score of, say, more than fifty, he would be excluded, unless he could persuade the others of the rightness of at least part of his cause, enough to get him down below fifty again! Ridiculous? Maybe, but this problem must find a solution!

5) *Some combination of the above.*

It may be that none of these solutions commends itself to you. That is all right, if you will expend your time and effort to address the problem.

Is there any hope that a solution to this problem will be found? We are not the first generation to recognize the difficulty. In 1787 J.P. Gabler attacked dogmatic (systematic) theology as being far removed from Scripture. He proposed that going back to studying the text of Scripture was the way ahead. Systematics must rest on biblical texts.

> The first part of Gabler's proposal, the rupturing of the link between biblical study and confessional application, was soon widely adopted, but the second part, that the results of such biblical theology should then be deployed in the construction of dogmatics, was largely ignored…[As a result] the drift of biblical theology was toward the increasingly atomistic, cut off from any obligation to traditional dogmatics.[7]

Once again we are seeing a revival of biblical or exegetical theology, a searching for the meaning of texts and books and testaments prior to or, more accurately, accompanying systematization. This time many conservatives and evangelicals are at the forefront of the effort. We must not let this opportunity be lost. The presence of strict subscription to creeds fosters fear, fear of being ostracized, in men who might otherwise tackle this problem. At first, questioning a creedal statement will require godly courage in such groups, but when done intelligently and prayerfully it will be worth the cost. The fearful trend in our day is to follow the battle cry: "Love unites, but doctrine divides!" Certainly we must emphasize love…and unashamedly! I would like to think that this paper is such a plea. But if this one-sided slogan were to prevail, it would mean the abandonment of truth in the church of Jesus Christ. Yet experience suggests that, humanly speaking, the fear inspired by our creedal stances keeps us from pursuing unity, both in love and in truth.

As I began this chapter, I set before you the facts we must wrestle with:

1) *Our creeds and confessions are one immense barrier to unity.*
2) *There is no easy or obvious way to cross this divide.*

Neither of these two things has changed in the time it took you to read this chapter. Perhaps, then, you will want to join me in this brief prayer: "May God grant us a marriage between exegesis and systematic theology resulting in greater unity in understanding his Word."

Is this too much to hope for? Not at all, given the nature of our God who holds men and opinions in his mighty hands. The truth is certain to prevail, but it will not do so automatically, without God-inspired effort. He will use sinful humans, opposing their own sinful subjectivity, to do his work.

10

BAPTISM AND THE UNITY OF CHRISTIANS

Among the differences that divide Christians, baptism looms very large. Unlike other doctrine and practices of the church, our differences on baptism fall along a number of lines at once. We seem unable to agree on any of the following: (1) mode of baptism, (2) proper candidates for baptism, (3) proper administrators for baptism and (4) effects of baptism.

Most agree on only two things: baptism requires water and baptism is appropriate at the outset (in some sense) of the Christian life. Apart from these marginal agreements the word "baptism" is a symbol without meaning—and this after 2000 years of use! Looked at in this way, "baptism" bears all the earmarks of a great tragedy. No wonder a few groups have ignored it altogether. Let us look at these differences.

MODE OF BAPTISM

Three "modes"[1] of baptism have been widely used among Christians: immersion, pouring and sprinkling. In immersion the candidate is

This essay first appeared in *Reformation & Revival Journal*, 8, No. 3 (Summer 1999), 101–110.

dipped under water. Variations include dipping either forward or backward and immersing the candidate either once in the name of the Trinity or three times, once for each person of the Trinity. These variations are themselves the subject of vigorous debate among some groups of Christians. The reason is not hard to find: Symbolism is involved. Each group reasonably contends that the symbol must agree, as far as possible, with the thing it signifies. The subject is further complicated by the possibility that baptism signifies more than one thing. Immersionists, for example, might contend for two meanings or more, including a thorough "drenching" with the Holy Spirit and the Christian's joint burial and resurrection with Jesus Christ.

Symbolism, of course, also enters into pouring and sprinkling. Those who practice pouring water over the head and body of the candidate often want to show, by a figure, the effect of the outpouring of the Spirit on believers. Others practice trine pouring, symbolizing our coming under the lordship of the Trinity. Those who sprinkle may be most interested in demonstrating the effect of cleansing from sin, using a mode that was prominent in the Old Testament for the washing away of guilt. Those who practice each of these modes point to texts and situations in the New Testament that bolster their views.[2]

PROPER CANDIDATES FOR BAPTISM

We are also divided on the question of who are proper candidates for baptism. Baptists hold that only those who can testify to believing in Christ ought to be baptized. Other Christians baptize infants and very young children. This is an enormous difference in itself, and it is further complicated by a lack of agreement among those who baptize infants over the grounds on which this ought to be done. I will come to this in discussing "Effects of baptism."

PROPER ADMINISTRATORS OF BAPTISM

The early church suffered several divisions in which the issue was the proper administrators for baptism.[3] In our century this question is still important among such groups as Landmark Baptists and Churches of

Christ. In the case of the Landmarkers, the point is that a proper church must immerse believers. In the Churches of Christ of the "non-additions" group, there is the conviction that other administrators will not require the proper views on baptism from the candidates.

EFFECTS OF BAPTISM

Here we reach the most critical point connected with baptism: its actual effect on the candidate who is baptized. What precisely does baptism do? How is a man, woman or infant different before and after baptism, or are they different at all? The variations here are tremendously important.

When the Roman Catholic priest baptizes, he believes that both original and actual sin are forgiven through the merits of Christ. The Reformers varied among themselves, and their heirs continue to differ. Lutherans hold that faith is necessary in the one baptized, but also insist that there is no reason why infants cannot exercise faith. This view, then, seems close to the view of the Roman Catholic Church as far as effects are concerned. The Calvinists have usually emphasized baptism's connection with what is called "covenant theology." In this view a person is assured of his or her interest in "the covenant" when baptized. Baptism in the case of infants, however, is variously explained so that its effects differ as far as forgiveness of sins is concerned. Some of the Reformed hold to forgiveness because of presumed faith in the infants, whereas others simply make baptism the entrance into the visible congregation of "believers and their seed."

Baptists do not usually think of baptism in terms of effects wrought in the believer. For them it is rather a badge of profession, showing the world that they have submitted to the lordship of Jesus Christ or, at the least, believed in him as Saviour.

THE WAY FORWARD

A glance at the differences over baptism shows the large amount of work we must do to eventually arrive at unity. This will be no easy task.

First, we must overcome our lethargy. We must fight the impulse to say, "We are so seriously divided, why bother?" Division among Christians is a product of sin. The sin is not the fact that we cannot agree, but the cause behind it, what theologians call "the noetic effects of sin." Sin has attacked our minds as well as our wills, our emotions and our bodies. In the face of sin we must throw down the gauntlet, not throw in the towel.

Second, we must seek to overcome our sinful pride. The conviction that we are right and others are wrong is, in itself, inevitable. If we seriously thought that our neighbour was right, our convictions would be his convictions and there would be no division between us. But satisfaction with our own convictions that paralyzes open-hearted discussion is wrong. We must re-examine our "certainties." We can get nowhere as long as we cannot conceive that we may be wrong.

Third, we must try to break the questions over baptism into more basic questions of biblical interpretation and historical practice. When we survey the opinions that divide us, the *effect of baptism* certainly takes first place. But the key here is an obvious one: the realistic language of Scripture. New Testament texts that describe baptism normally speak of it as effecting some important spiritual change in or for those who are baptized. Through most of church history this language has been taken literally. Is that the correct way to take it? Does baptism bring with it the remission of sins (Acts 2:38)? Did Paul really "wash away" his sins in baptism (Acts 22:16)? Or are these statements of what baptism symbolizes? Two things need to be said. To start with, we must treat Scripture (in this respect) like any other document; it must be allowed to speak for itself. This suggests that the burden of proof lies on those who find in this language a figurative sense.[4] Such men and women must make their case from the New Testament before they can expect others to listen. But that is not all. Once that case has been carefully laid out, others must listen as sympathetically as possible. Only then can genuine discussion go forward.

Fourth, we must come to a biblical view of the relative amount of weight to be given to the Old Testament and New Testament in our thinking. Here is the great stumbling block to agreement among Baptists and Presbyterians who are evangelicals. Here the burden of proof falls on those who find their baptismal doctrine in the Old Testament rather than the New Testament. And here Baptists must try to listen sympathetically to what their paedobaptist brothers have to say.

Fifth, we must seek to read history honestly, and not simply to bolster our own prejudices. History outside the Bible cannot determine our doctrine, but it can often show us the understanding of "the Fathers" who handled the Scriptures in the following centuries. We must not follow them slavishly, but their writings exist for our instruction.

HAVE WE MADE ANY PROGRESS?

As greatly as we are divided, there are, here and there, signs that things are not as bad as they once were. Some of the evidence, slight though it is, follows.

In 1977, InterVarsity Press issued *The Water that Divides*, an irenic look at the baptism debate.[5] Here two participants, apparently co-authoring each chapter and section rather than writing alternately, discuss "Baptism & Scripture," "Baptism & History" and "Baptism Today." In the closing section, they suggest ways for Baptists and paedobaptists to work together, even in the local church setting. Whether through the influence of this book or not, a relatively few churches are trying to live with diverse views and practices about baptism. An example of such a church is Community Evangelical Fellowship of Moscow, Idaho. Douglas Wilson writes of his church:

> We receive both baptistic and paedobaptistic households into membership. We practice both infant baptism and baptism upon profession of faith. We are able to do this because the membership of our church is reckoned by household, and because we all share a strong sense of the covenantal identity of each household, whether baptist or paedobaptist.
>
> As part of this cooperation agreement, we have stated the

following in our constitution: "Because of our commitment to the unity of the Spirit in the bond of peace" (Ephesians 4:3), and because of our shared commitment to the practice of household membership...these differences have been procedurally resolved between us. We have agreed to work together in this way until such time as the Lord brings us to one mind on the subject of baptism.[6]

Several Baptists have written books on baptism that adopt "covenant theology," the justification for paedobaptism used by many Presbyterians.[7] Nevertheless, they have not conceded much else to their opponents. More remarkable were the attacks on paedobaptism by Karl Barth from within a paedobaptist denomination.

From within paedobaptist ranks has come *Baptism in the Early Church*, an earnest endeavour to read the writers of the first four centuries objectively. The book of twenty-six chapters and a bibliography opens with a discussion of the use of church history by modern scholars and continues by discussing the church fathers through Theodore of Mopsuestia (A.D. 350–428). It closes with a look at early Christian art and the authors' conclusions.[8]

An interesting development, not initially intended to settle differences about baptism, has come in a recent (1998) joint venture between Reformed Baptists and Westminster Seminary in California (Westminster West) that enables Baptist students to receive instruction out of their own tradition on matters where Baptists and Presbyterians differ. Both groups see this as an attempt at expressing Christian unity. The possibilities here for interaction between two differing traditions are promising.

CONCLUSIONS

It is easy to ask, "Why don't we all get together?" It is much harder to accomplish. Baptism illustrates the problem, with no simple solutions in sight and few efforts being put forth to eliminate our differences. The large number of variations between us makes reconciling them seem like a daunting task. Before the age of the computer, mathematical problems existed that were so vast that they were left untouched. Baptism seems to present a similar dilemma. Given the truth of God's providence, one might reason as follows: If baptism were a question of central importance, as many think, surely the Lord would have led us to basic unity about it. This line of thought could be bolstered by noting that the discussion about baptism is a discussion about a ceremony, and ceremonies are clearly de-emphasized in the New Testament. That fact is crystal clear when one compares the multitude of rites and ceremonies under the Mosaic economy with the very few commanded for Christians.

Already in the Old Testament, in fact, the prophets felt the large relative difference between ceremonial and moral precepts.

> Thus says the Lord, "Stand by the ways and see and ask for the ancient paths, where the good way is, and walk in it; and you shall find rest to your souls. But they said, 'We will not walk *in it*'…But they said, 'We will not listen'…Your burnt offerings are not acceptable, And your sacrifices are not pleasing to me" (Jeremiah 6:16–20).

What is God's point here? *Those who ignore morality and godliness must stop their punctilious keeping of his ceremonies.* But notice this: We cannot even imagine him saying the opposite, "Away with your love for me and your personal integrity, unless you carefully offer your sacrifices!" Were the sacrifices not important? Of course, they were, but compared with godliness in the heart they were nothing. God himself had instituted them, but as important as they were, they were not to be compared with spiritual life.

So then, is baptism relatively unimportant? As attractive as this option is, many strongly deny it. They remind us that there is more than a hint of a relation between circumcision and baptism in the New Testament. (The extent of that relation is one of the things strongly contested, but few deny it outright.) And they insist that whatever was true of burnt offerings and sacrifices under the Old Testament, those who refused circumcision were cut off from God's ancient people (Genesis 17:10–14). The same, they tell us, goes for baptism today.

So the differences remain. Is it too much to suggest that those who feel most strongly about these differences are most obliged to seek their resolution? Surely the Lord would be pleased to see us pray for heartfelt reconciliation. Who knows but that he will have mercy on us and bless us?

Perhaps some day a writer of historical theology will write *A History of the Dialogue on Baptism*. Let us hope and pray that the day he sets pen to paper will not be too far away.

11

PREACHING
THE KINGDOM OF GOD

Not long ago I had a visit from the Jehovah's Witnesses. After we had talked a bit, one of them asked me, "How would you define the kingdom of God?" As you may know, the kingdom is one of their favourite themes. I gave my answer and after some further discussion they left. Does the subject of God's kingdom have the same interest for most Christians as it does for the Jehovah's Witnesses? It should. Why? Because understanding God's kingdom—in the broad terms with which I will treat it here—offers a framework for preaching and grasping the ongoing program of God.

Two things, particularly, make such understanding important to us. First, our Lord taught us to pray, "Thy kingdom come, Thy will be done, On earth as it is in heaven" (Matthew 6:10). Unless we are content with vain repetition, we will want to know what we are praying for. That is doubly true because the Lord Jesus did not leave us large numbers of subjects for prayer. This prayer, then, must be important. We cannot help being interested in its meaning.

This essay first appeared in *Reformation & Revival Journal*, 9, No. 1 (Winter 2000), 45–56.

Second, we see that the message preached in the Gospels is the message of "the kingdom of God" or, in Matthew's Gospel, "the kingdom of heaven," where "heaven" is used as a synonym for God. (Compare "heaven knows" and "God knows" in profane English.) Since this is the message of the Gospels, we dare not ignore it.

THE MEANING OF THE WORD "KINGDOM"

Let us start by reviewing the meaning of the word *kingdom*. In modern English kingdom most often means a realm or territory ruled over by a king. In the Bible it often has the same meaning. In a vision Satan showed the Lord Jesus "all the kingdoms of the world and their glory," and offered them to Jesus in return for worshipping him (Matthew 4:8–9). If we ask, "What was it that Jesus saw?" most likely the answer is a vast array of territories that Satan claimed to rule. "Look at all these countries! They are mine," Satan said in effect, "but they will be yours—every inch of them!"

In Scripture, however, kingdom often means something else, something like royal rule, reign, power, authority or sovereignty. When Paul writes in Colossians 1:13 that God "delivered us from the domain [Greek "authority"] of darkness, and transferred us to the kingdom of His beloved Son," he does not mean that God moved us from one place to another. Not at all! He means he took us out from under the reign of Satan and brought us under the kingship of Jesus Christ. So when we read of the "kingdom of God," we may translate this "God's kingship" or "the sovereignty of God." When we pray, "Thy kingdom come," we are praying, "God, bring your sovereignty to this world!" Again, kingdom means rule, reign or sovereignty.

PROBLEM: HAS GOD NOT ALWAYS BEEN SOVEREIGN?

If you have read the previous paragraph closely, however, a red flag may have gone up in your mind. I can imagine you saying to me, "Has God not always been sovereign over this world? How can we be praying for something that already exists?" These are good questions. Let us see if we can understand how God can be sovereign and yet urge us to pray for his sovereignty in the future.

When God created man and woman and placed them in Eden, two things were true. First, Adam and Eve obeyed God at the outset, and so did everything else. Second, Adam and Eve and everything that he made served God's purposes—everything without exception. That is what made Eden such a wonderful place. It was Paradise. Let us put this down in point form:

1) *Every creature obeyed God.*
2) *Every creature served God's purposes.*

But then something happened. Man disobeyed God, and God cast them out of Eden. This brought the state John Milton described as "Paradise Lost." Paul tells us that the whole creation was upset by man's disobedience (Romans 8:19–23). Number 1 above was no longer true. Adam and Eve no longer obeyed the Lord. Human sin made it impossible to say, "Every creature obeyed God."

But that raises the question: What about point number 2? Can we still say, "Every creature *serves* the purposes of God"? Oddly enough, the answer is yes. Men are now disobedient. They do not do what God commands. But that is not the whole story. They still serve the purposes of God, as really as Adam and Eve did before they sinned. How can this be? Let us see if we can give a scriptural answer to this question.

There are at least two things in the Bible called "the will of God." One of these is the commands God gives. When God says, "Do this!" we call his demand "his will." Here is a sentence that uses "God's will" in this way: "It is God's will that we love him with all our hearts." No Christian will argue with this use of the phrase "God's will." Every Christian will agree that the sentence we just read is true. God's command to love him is God's will for us. Theologians have called this God's *preceptive* will, the will we find in his precepts or commands.

Something else is also called "God's will" in Scripture, the things God has made up his mind will happen in this world. James gives us an example of this use:

> Come now, you who say, "Today or tomorrow, we shall go to such and such a city, and spend a year there and engage in business and make a profit." Yet you do not know what your life will be like tomorrow. You are just a vapor that appears for a little while and then vanishes away. Instead you ought to say, "If the Lord wills, we shall live and also do this or that" (James 4:13–15).

Here James tells us to often use the phrase, "If the Lord wills!" We are not independent beings who do whatever we choose. God is sovereign over us. We can do nothing that he does not either cause or permit. Now if you ask the question, "Why does God allow some things and not others?" the answer is he allows what serves his purposes. Anything else he prevents. There are no exceptions to this rule. Of course you will not want to take my word for this, but we will see that the Bible makes it plain.

Paul tells us that God "works all things after the counsel of His will" (Ephesians 1:11). Scripture illustrates this in many ways. We recall Joseph's speech to his brothers after their father's death. Fearing the worst, the brothers pled with Joseph to forgive them for their selling him into Egypt. But Joseph said to them, "Do not be afraid, for am I in God's place? And as for you, you meant evil against me, but God meant it for good in order to bring about this present result, to preserve many people alive" (Genesis 50:19–20).

Being sold into slavery served two sets of purposes in Joseph's life. His brothers sold him to be rid of him, and their purpose was served. But God allowed it for his own purpose, to save the people of Israel alive. Unless the grace of God later intervened, the brothers would answer for their evil purpose. But that did not keep them from serving God's purpose. They did so as really as if that was all they wanted to do!

The highest and best illustration of this truth is the cross of

Jesus Christ. No one supposes that the enemies who killed him were moved by a desire to further the purposes of God. Not in the least! But that is what they did. If we ask the question, "What is the greatest sin ever committed?" certainly this sin must be high on that list. But if we ask, "What is the greatest source of blessing of anything that has happened in this world?" we see that the answer is the same in each case, the killing of Jesus Christ. God's purpose was served in the midst of their sin. In fact, if God does not rule over sin, he may rule in Mars or Jupiter or Venus, but not in this world. Everything humanity does has the shadow of sin cast across it. The sovereignty of God is a mere name if he is not sovereign over sin. We see this again in Paul's experience with Satan (2 Corinthians 12:1–10). There Paul calls his thorn in the flesh "a messenger of Satan" (verse 7). But if we ask Paul what its purpose was, he tells us nothing about Satan's motivation. Instead he describes God's purpose:

> [B]ecause of the surpassing greatness of the revelations, for this reason, to keep me from exalting myself, there was given me a thorn in the flesh, a messenger of Satan to buffet me—*to keep me from exalting myself!* (2 Corinthians 12:7, *italics mine*)

As far as the record is concerned, we are left totally in the dark about Satan's purpose. God's purpose is all that counts!

Before we go on, let us review the effect of the Fall. Before the Fall two things were true:

1) *Every creature obeyed God.*
   His *preceptive will* was carried out.
2) *Every creature served God's purposes.*
   His *decretive will* was done.

Since the Fall, men are disobedient, but as far as God's purposes are concerned, all creatures continue to serve the purposes of God. Sin eliminated the first point but left the second intact. If we look over the whole span of history for a moment we will see that in Eden God's will, in both senses, was done. Now it is not. Men do not obey God, though they continue to serve his purposes. In eternity future, however, we will know "*Paradise Regained*" (to borrow another title from Milton). Then men will obey God once more, and they will continue to serve his purposes. Why will this happen? Because God will exercise his *kingship* to make it that way. We will obey him just as the unfallen angels in heaven obey. That explains why we pray, "Thy kingdom come, Thy will be done, On earth as it is in heaven." In heaven, God's commands and God's decrees are both carried out. Sin destroyed the marriage between these two, but when sin is destroyed God will unite them again.

WHAT ABOUT GOD'S KINGSHIP NOW?

Since God has been sovereign throughout history, he has been bringing about his purposes. We may ask where we can see this, we see it in everything that happens. But occasionally we can see it dramatically in the destruction of the wicked. The flood, in which vast numbers of mankind were killed, illustrates this. He has also exercised his wisdom and sovereignty in creating outposts of righteousness, starting with Adam and Eve and continuing through Noah, the patriarchs and Israel, both as a whole and in its remnants. All of these obeyed God and kept his precepts, to a greater or lesser extent. These events of judgment and mercy suggested and pictured a giant step forward that God would bring about in "the last days."

When will God assert his kingship in this fuller way? When will the last days arrive?

Not too many years ago, the popular answer to this question went something like this: The last days will come when the millennium arrives (*or*, when we are ushered into eternity). In other words, the last days will begin with the return of Christ. But recently another answer has become evident from Scripture. The last days began with the complex of events connected with the first appearance of Christ. The writer to the Hebrews makes this point in starting his book. "God, after He spoke long ago to the fathers in the prophets in many portions and in many ways, in these last days has spoken to us in His Son" (Hebrews 1:1–2a). For this writer, the last days have already come.

This means that God's kingdom began at the same time. We should not be surprised at this, because both John the Baptist and Jesus preached the coming of God's kingdom in a very short time. John said, "Repent, for the kingdom of God is at hand" (Matthew 3:2). Mark gives Jesus' words as, "The time is fulfilled, and the kingdom of God is at hand; repent and believe in the gospel" (Mark 1:15). Note the reference to fulfillment. Jesus' hearers were living on the brink of the kingdom of God which had been promised for the last days. This message caught the ears of many of those who heard it, because it was the very thing they were looking for. Later Mark cites Joseph of Arimathea as an example of such a man. He describes him as "a prominent member of the Council [Sanhedrin], who himself was waiting for the kingdom of God" (Mark 15:43).

Earlier I wrote, "The last days began with the complex of events connected with the first appearance of Christ." If that failed to locate an exact moment for the coming of God's rule, it was no accident. The moment is difficult to pinpoint. Many have seen the kingdom, that is, the authority and rule of God, revealed in the activity of Christ in the Gospels, and with good reason! No one before him ever displayed the authority of God over men, nature and death in the way the Lord Jesus did. It seems unwise, then, to exclude this activity from the coming of the kingdom. Nevertheless, the giant step forward in the kingship of God seems to have come at the exaltation of Jesus. At that point he can say, "All authority has been given to Me in heaven and on earth" (Matthew 28:18). The Messianic King, promised in ages past, has come and is now exercising his reign on earth! Man once ruled as God's prime minister in Eden. Man now rules again on earth (and in heaven), in the person of Jesus Christ!

> [God] left nothing that is not subject to [man]. But now we do not yet see all things subjected to him. But we do see Him

who has been made for a little while lower than the angels, namely, Jesus, because of the suffering of death crowned with glory and honour... (Hebrews 2:8–9).

God's King has come. He has been crowned. All things are not yet subject to mankind generally, but they are subject to him. Redeemed humanity will join him in ruling, when he has completed the task of "bringing many sons to glory" (Hebrews 2:10). In the meantime, we rule in our representative Head.

The Old Testament, however, promises a new heavens and a new earth, a new creation. Is that promise strictly future? More than that, if it is strictly future, how is that consistent with the arrival of the kingship of God in the past? And, if it is not strictly future, how is it seen in any of the events connected to the appearance of Jesus Christ two thousand years ago?

As we have seen, God has always been sovereign. To speak of the coming of his sovereignty or kingship is to speak relatively of "a giant step forward" in the progress he is making in returning men to his own moral likeness. Obviously that work is not yet done. It is not even started in those who are yet to be saved, and it is not done in me or in you. To speak of God's kingship coming is like speaking of grace coming (John 1:17) or faith coming (Galatians 3:25). All three have existed throughout history. That does not mean, however, that the new creation is strictly future. It too has begun. How? By the creation of the new nation made up of God's elect, the church. Do you remember Paul's language in 2 Corinthians 5:17? He speaks of a "new creation." The NASV translates this, "Therefore if any man is in Christ, he is a new creature." It is equally possible to translate this verse as follows, "Therefore if any man is in Christ, there is the new creation," that is, the new creation has begun in that its citizens are being joined to Jesus Christ to form the new people of God. The thought is captured in the New English Bible: "When anyone is united to Christ, there is a new world; the old order is gone, and a new order has already begun." The Lord Jesus now rules over the nation that will populate eternity.

Notice how Peter develops this idea at Pentecost:

> Therefore having been exalted to the right hand of God, and having received from the Father the promise of the Holy Spirit, He has poured forth this which you both see and hear. For it was not David who ascended into heaven, but he himself says: "The Lord said to my Lord, 'Sit at my right hand, until I make thine enemies a footstool for thy feet.' " Therefore let all the house of Israel know for certain that God has made Him both Lord and Christ—this Jesus whom you crucified (Acts 2:33–36).

Jesus, who is both Lord and Christ, shares the rule with his Father. Peter's listeners recognized the impact of this. Though they were Israelites, they were not yet citizens of the new creation. Sensing their lack—though probably not precisely in these terms—they cried out with fear, "Brethren, what shall we do?" (Acts 2:37). In essence Peter said, "Bow the knee to God's King; give your allegiance to Jesus Christ." Peter might have adopted the words of Paul (had they been written when he spoke):

> Therefore also God highly exalted Him, and bestowed on Him the name which is above every name, that at the name of Jesus every knee should bow, of those who are in heaven and on earth, and under the earth, and that every tongue should confess that Jesus Christ is Lord, to the glory of God the Father (Philippians 2:9–11).

In saying these things both Peter and Paul were preaching the kingdom of God. The kingdom was inaugurated with the coming of Christ as God's King. It runs through the age in which we live. In preaching the gospel, the Apostles used the keys that let men into God's kingdom. As the book of Acts closes we see Paul still tirelessly "testifying about the kingdom of God" (Acts 28:23) and preaching the kingdom of God (Acts 28:31).

CHRIST COMES IN TWO STAGES

Before the Fall of man two things were true:

1) *Every creature obeyed God.*
   His *preceptive will* was carried out.
2) *Every creature served God's purposes.*
   His *decretive will* was done.

The Fall pried these two things apart. Disobedience entered and has remained to characterize human life. Nevertheless all things still carry out the purposes of God. When we pray, "Thy kingdom come. Thy will be done, on earth as it is in heaven," we are praying that God will create a new world in which these two things will come together once more. They remained together in heaven; they must be reunited on earth.

How will this finally be accomplished? The second coming of Christ will finish the work. We glimpse the completion in the book of Revelation:

> And the seventh angel sounded; and there arose loud voices in heaven saying, "The kingdom of the world has become the kingdom of our Lord and of His Christ; and He will reign forever and ever" (Revelation 11:15).

What are the "loud voices in heaven" referring to? Their words might have been spoken at the ascension of our Lord when "all authority in heaven and on earth" (Matthew 28:18) became his. It was then that his reign was inaugurated. That was his coronation day. But the following verses in Revelation are an inspired commentary on verse 15:

> And the twenty-four elders, who sit on their thrones before God, fell on their faces and worshiped God, saying, "We give Thee thanks, O Lord God, the Almighty, who art and who wast, because Thou hast taken Thy great power and hast

begun to reign. And the nations were enraged, and Thy wrath came, and the time came for the dead to be judged, and the time to give their reward to Thy bond-servants the prophets and to the saints and to those who fear Thy name, the small and the great, and to destroy those who destroy the earth" (Revelation 11:16–18).

So then, the coming of God's kingship will not be complete until judgment comes, with destruction and reward. Sin will be banished from the new earth forever. Happily, obedience will be restored completely. Once more, God's preceptive will (his commands) and his decretive will (his ongoing purposes) will be reunited. His will once more will be done in earth as it is in heaven.

Every preacher of the gospel of Jesus Christ is thus a preacher of the kingdom of God. The gospel is the gospel of the kingdom. It is the exercise of God's kingship through Jesus Christ that even as you read this chapter he is capturing men and women and making them citizens of God's kingdom. In a sense, that has been God's program in every age, as we have seen. The kingship of God unites his purposes in history. What has been true throughout history is preeminently true today. The last days have come in that the giant step forward appeared in the coming of Jesus Christ. We do not await its appearance but its completion. Hence we continue to pray, "Thy kindom come, the will be done on earth as it is in heaven!"

12

ARE YOU DISCOURAGED IN PREACHING THE GOSPEL?

You know this already, but let us just remind ourselves again at the beginning of this chapter: evangelism is difficult and unpredictable work. Where there are brave and far-reaching efforts to win men to Christ, two problems arise. First, the results are always less than we hoped for. Second, they are usually less than they seemed to be at the outset. These two problems sometimes dampen our zeal to point men to Christ. They should not, but they do.

I think it will help us to see that the Lord Jesus faced these same problems. After he fed five thousand, the crowds dogged his footsteps. Listen to what happened between him and them:

> When they found Him on the other side of the lake, they asked Him, "Rabbi, when did You get here?"
>
> Jesus answered, "I tell you the truth, you are looking for Me, not because you saw miraculous signs but because you ate the loaves and had your fill. Do not work for food that

This essay first appeared in *Reformation & Revival Journal*, 1, No. 4 (Fall 1992), 53–60.

spoils, but for food that endures to eternal life, which the Son of Man will give you. On Him God the Father has placed His seal of approval."

They asked Him, "What must we do to do the works God requires?" (John 6:25–28).

To begin with, most teachers would be pleased to have others follow them around. Is that not what teaching and preaching are all about, having people to speak to? And the more the better! The Lord, however, looked for godly motives. He knew that these men had failed to understand him. They had had their bellies filled. To them, that was more important than his teaching, and much more important than his person. That, in turn, must have tempted our Lord to be discouraged. Was all his incomparable teaching in vain? It might have seemed that way. Jesus had to tell these men that there is other food to seek beyond the food that feeds our flesh.

Let us look back to see how bleak the situation was. Verse 28 looks as if it contains a ray of light. We would be glad to have someone ask us, "What must I do to do the works God requires?" When we keep on reading, however, we find that the ray of light was more apparent than real:

Jesus answered, "The work of God is this: to believe in the One He has sent."

So they asked Him, "What miraculous sign then will You give that we may see it and believe You? What will You do? Our forefathers ate the manna in the desert; as it is written: 'He gave them bread from heaven to eat'" (John 6:29–31).

Jesus answered these men graciously. He told them that they must believe in him. They understood what he said, but they wanted to quibble. "How about a sign from heaven?" they say. And they imply more: "Just give us that sign and we will be ready to believe in you."

It is hard not to feel that their answer is impudent. They may have expected the manna to come from heaven again when the

Messiah came. Many in that day did think so. But in speaking of the Lord's miracle as nothing, they treated him very rudely. More than that, the fact that they went after him across the lake shows the value they attached to it. When it came to their bellies, they were willing enough to follow him. Once more the Lord might have been greatly discouraged.

When we read on, we see that things did not get better:

> Jesus said to them, "I tell you the truth, It is not Moses who has given you the bread from heaven, but it is My Father who gives you the true bread from heaven. For the bread of God is He who comes down from heaven and gives life to the world."
>
> "Sir," they said, "from now on give us this bread."
>
> Then Jesus declared, "I am the bread of life. He who comes to Me will never go hungry, and he who believes in Me will never be thirsty. But as I told you, you have seen Me and still do not believe" (John 6:32–36).

Jesus explained that he himself was the bread for men's souls. Verse 34 looks promising, but it seems to mean no more than this: "We want bread! Give us bread!" Their denseness was as great as their impudence. This part of the discussion ends with Jesus telling them plainly that they are unbelievers: "You have seen Me and still do not believe."

Now is the time for us to stop and to ask the Lord some key questions: "Lord, if you with all your gifts were unable to bring these men to faith, what hope is there for us when we set out to evangelize? Can we make you more attractive than you were when you walked here in the flesh?" The story to the point where we quit reading seems to require questions like these.

That is not all.

At this point we might suppose that the Lord himself would have been fully discouraged. After all, if we met that kind of opposition we might remind ourselves that we are mere men. But this is the Lord Jesus. If he can do nothing, how can any man be saved?

So we might ask two more questions: "Lord, what hope do you have of doing anything with men like these? Are you not ready to give up?" He gives his answer as we read on:

> All that the Father gives Me will come to Me, and whoever comes to Me I will never drive away. For I have come down from heaven not to do My will but to do the will of Him who sent Me. And this is the will of Him who sent Me, that I shall lose none of all that He has given Me, but raise them up at the last day. For My Father's will is that everyone who looks to the Son and believes in Him shall have eternal life, and I will raise him up at the last day (John 6:37–40).

How does Jesus answer our questions? Why is he sure that his ministry will not be in vain? Here is his answer: "All that the Father gives Me will come to Me!" The God who promised the Lord Jesus kinsmen whom no one could number will be as good as his word. The answer to the wickedness of human nature is not found in human eloquence or attractiveness. It is not found even in the miraculous. The answer is found in God! God will see to it. The sovereign, almighty God!

It is important now to see that this is not an isolated experience on Jesus' part. What he says and does here is typical of his words and actions elsewhere. Let us take his words first, the short and powerful statement in Matthew 11 in which the Lord speaks to both God and man. Here is the record:

> At that time Jesus said, "I praise You, Father, Lord of heaven and earth, because You have hidden these things from the wise and learned, and revealed them to little children. Yes, Father, for this was Your good pleasure.
>
> "All things have been committed to Me by My Father. No one knows the Son except the Father, and no one knows the Father except the Son and those to whom the Son chooses to reveal Him."

"Come to Me, all you who are weary and burdened, and I will give you rest. Take My yoke upon you and learn from me, for I am gentle and humble in heart, and you will find rest for your souls. For My yoke is easy and My burden is light" (Matthew 11:25–30).

What we have here is this: Evangelism brought into the closest possible relation to the sovereignty of God. Matthew 11:25 and 26 tell us that the Father controls the revelation of his truth. From some—the wise and learned—he hides it. To others—little children—he reveals it. On what basis? His good pleasure! Nor is that all. To remove all doubt from Jesus' meaning, verse 27 repeats how much the whole process of coming to God and Christ are under their control. "No one knows the Son...and no one knows the Father..." except by direct revelations from one of these two persons.

Does that inhibit evangelism? Not at all! Matthew 11:28 to 30 immediately launch into the most unfettered invitation: Come to Jesus Christ, and be saved! How can this be? The answer is clear: The power expressed in verses 25 to 27 is exercised to make the invitation in verses 28 to 30 effective. Once we grasp that fact, the words of our Lord fit nicely together. Before we see that, we are bound to be uncomfortable with one side of this truth or the other.

We may also see the recognition of God's sovereignty in the things the Lord Jesus did. His actions as well as his words bear witness to the sovereignty of God in salvation. Take, for example, Jesus' dealings with the rich young ruler who asked him what good thing he would have to do to inherit eternal life. The next time you read the passage (Matthew 19:16ff), ask yourself this question: How did Jesus fail to win this man to himself? See if the answer is not this: Jesus seemed more eager to avoid false profession than to clinch a decision. Does it not seem that he keeps throwing stumbling blocks in the young man's way? First, Jesus tells him to keep the commandments. Would you tell a seeker that? Then Jesus tells him to sell everything that he has and give his money away. Would you tell a seeker that? The Lord Jesus did, and we might have predicted the result. The man turned away, never—so far as we know—to come back to Christ. Who would dare to do such a thing without confidence in the sovereignty of God?

Did I say that we might have predicted the result? Yes, I said that, but, I was wrong, dead wrong. The fact is, the whole result was in the hands of God. No one could have predicted the outcome. As Jesus soon said to his disciples, "With man this is impossible, but with God all things are possible" (Matthew 19:26). God can save anybody if he wills to do so. The hope of evangelistic preaching lies in this great truth. Jesus' actions, as well as his words, bear this out.

Let me give you one more example from the public preaching of the Lord Jesus, his discourse in Luke 14 on the cost of discipleship. We read:

> Large crowds were traveling with Jesus, and turning to them He said: "If anyone comes to Me and does not hate his father and mother, his wife and children, his brother and sisters—yes, even his own life—he cannot be My disciple. And anyone who does not carry his cross and follow after Me cannot be my disciple."
>
> "Any of you who does not give up everything that he has cannot be My disciple" (Luke 14:25–27,33).

Is this the kind of evangelism that we feel comfortable with? Would we not be tempted to say (if the speaker were not Jesus Christ!), "You can catch more flies with honey than with vinegar?" Someone may object, however, that this call is not to salvation but to something beyond salvation. Salvation, in that view, is a first step that many take, but discipleship is a higher step or a deeper commitment to the Lord Jesus.

I do not think it is possible to find that distinction in this text. Luke 14:25 says that Jesus spoke these words to the *large crowds* that traveled with him. Such a distinction, even if it were true, would have been lost on them. These men and women could hear nothing in these words but a call for decision. Would they follow him, or would they turn back? That was the question.

Why would Jesus evangelize in such an apparently negative way? The answer is clear, is it not? He was not leaning upon his personal attractiveness or the beauty of his words to gain his followers. Rather, he knew his dependence on a sovereign God, and he acted consistently with what he knew. It was indeed possible to gain false followers by the sheer power of his personality or his presentation; but, real disciples could only come to him if the Father brought them.

Finally, here is the lesson for us: Discouragement in evangelism is both unnecessary and wrong. *Unnecessary?* Yes, because the Father has a plan that will be carried out. *Wrong?* Yes, because our only purpose is to carry out the Father's plan. The Lord Jesus himself is our grand example. "I have come down from heaven," he once said, "not to do My will but to do the will of Him who sent Me" (John 6:38). That is all, nothing less, but also nothing more.

That brings us back to the two problems I mentioned when we began. What were they? First, the results of our evangelism are always less than we hoped for. Second, they are usually less than they seemed to be at the outset. As a man, the Lord Jesus may have hoped to bring everyone he met to believe in him. "Come to Me," he said to a multitude. The least we can say is this: Surely he would have been happy if all of them had really come. They did not all come, however. Most turned away from him—forever!

He faced the other problem, too. Many seemed to come to him at first who later proved to be untrue. But neither of these disheartened him.

They should not dampen our spirits either. For the same God who held men in his hands in that day holds them today. More than that, he is still giving them into the hands of Christ. Not one of his elect will get away. They will all come! Often one by one. Sometimes two by two. And sometimes, in seasons of wide-scale awakening, in great multitudes. The Father has a plan and he continues to pursue it. And it shall be done!

Go on, then, with your work of telling men and women and children about Christ. If you are a teacher, set forth the Lord Jesus to your pupils. If you are a parent, earnestly lay Christ before your children. If you are a preacher of the gospel, preach Christ and him as crucified! Many will not come; we know that. But we know something else also: Christ will get a people from every tribe, tongue, kindred and nation. Many will later turn away, but our Lord Jesus will have his new nation after all. The work is the work of God.

With men this is impossible. But take heart, for with God all things are possible!

13

MOTIVES
FOR EVANGELISM

Motives are tricky things. There are two pitfalls in looking too closely at them. First, there is the danger of unhealthy introspection. Take the man, for instance, who thinks he has discovered a bit of pride in his heart that he was not previously aware of. How will he react? Well, he might say, "Yes, I can see that it was pride that led me to take the course I took, but at least it is humble of me to admit it." C.S. Lewis has told us:

> There is one vice of which no man in the world is free; which every one in the world loathes when he sees it in someone else; and of which hardly any people, except Christians, ever imagine that they are guilty themselves …The vice I am talking of is Pride or Self-Conceit…[1]

If Lewis is right—and I think he is—our friend might seem to have good reason to congratulate himself on ferreting out his pride

This essay first appeared in *Reformation & Revival Journal*, 8, No. 2 (Spring 1999), 157–167.

before it poisoned his entire life.

But this kind of introspection is endless. Yes, he was humble in admitting his pride, but then he was more than a little proud of his humility. Of course, he could then humbly admit his second bout with pride and pat himself on the back. But that would call for another rebuke, *ad infinitum* and *ad nauseum*. Soon our friend would drown in his obsession with the purity of his motives. Better to have said, "I was proud," and gotten on with it.

The second pitfall is closely related to the first. If we become obsessed with our motives we may be paralyzed into inaction. Our friend ran that risk. Had he kept up his pursuit, some critic would no doubt have accused him of navel-gazing. And there would have been more than a little truth in the accusation.

But motives are immensely important. There is a sense in which they are the only things that are important. The Puritan, Richard Sibbes, has been quoted as saying, "God takes the intention for the action." In other words, if the movement of the heart is right, God is pleased with what we do. I suppose that someone will remind me of the proverb that says, "The road to hell is paved with good intentions." And so it is. But the proverb does not address the same situation we are thinking of. It is a rebuke to those who intend to do nothing now. Tomorrow, yes; but today, no. In speaking of motives for evangelism, we are speaking to those who want to get on with the job of telling men and women about Christ. They are the people who need to ask simply, "Why do I want to do this?" The answers they give to that question will reveal whether or not their evangelism is pleasing to God.

The question, "Why do I want to evangelize?" has three kinds of answers. There are (1) bad answers, (2) at least one insufficient answer and (3) one fully satisfactory answer.

Can there be a really *bad* reason to evangelize? Let me tell you a story, and you can be the judge. We will pretend that I made this story up, since it has been some time since I read this man's biography and I can no longer vouch for every detail. Think of it only as an illustration; the effect will be the same.

Years ago a pastor who was later to become famous was about to be voted out of his church. I do not remember the reason, but it is not relevant to my story. What to do?—that was the question.

It was not long before he had the answer. Why not evangelize, bring new people into the church? Then, when it came time to vote, his new converts would vote for him and he could keep his pulpit. He may have reminded himself that his enemies would surely turn up a good crowd of members who no longer attended to vote against him. Would it not be a case of wisely fighting fire with fire? There could not be anything wrong with that, could there? In any case, his plan worked. Many made professions of faith in Christ, and they helped him retain his pulpit. He went on, as I said, to become a famous leader of men.

We may say of this story what Paul said of some preaching in his day, "The important thing is that in every way, whether from false motives or true, Christ is preached. And because of this I rejoice" (Philippians 1:18). Apparently Paul held that Christ could be glorified and men and women won to him even when the motives of the preachers were corrupt. If so, since he wrote by inspiration, we must agree with him. But he did not commend corrupt motives. A bad motive is wrong, even if good comes from what is done. Pleasing God with our motives is a chief business of Christians. So Paul laid his finger on the sore spot: "false motives." And we must listen to what he wrote.

"But, after all," someone may say," this kind of thing cannot be very common. How many preachers go out to preach the gospel in order to keep from being voted out of their churches?" The point is well made, I imagine; surely this does not often happen.

Let the story stand, however, for all the false motives that move men to preach Christ. Are there no pastors who preach Christ with the hope of having more converts to boast of than others have? Are there no evangelists who preach with the idea of making a name for themselves and their ministries? Are there no Sunday School teachers who are prompted to greater efforts by the prospect of winning a contest and receiving recognition for themselves and their class or department? You will see here, I think, the possibility of endless wrong motives for preaching and teaching the gospel of Christ.

Let us turn now to an *insufficient* motive, a reason that is good in itself though not powerful enough to sustain the work of Christ over lifetimes and centuries. Let us think of the motive of concern for the lost. Here we are dealing with a motive that is good and right and necessary. A man without concern for lost men and women around him has no business calling himself a Christian, much less thinking of himself as doing the work of an evangelist. Do the cries of the perishing mean nothing to you? May God have mercy on your soul! Have you received forgiveness and yet care nothing that others receive it too? Then you are an ungrateful wretch, deceived about the pardon of which you boast. But that is not the whole story.

Concern for the lost is an insufficient motive because in itself it would not have sustained the work of even one generation. The reason is this: Many of the men for whom Christians are concerned will do all in their power to repel our witness. To put it bluntly, they will tell us straight out that they want none of what we have to offer.

Now, of course, I do not mean that every person to whom we speak of Christ will respond in that way; but, the fact remains that many will do so. Sometimes they will do so as individuals, sometimes as ethnic groups and sometimes as adherents of false religions. When this happens, the Christian will need more than a feeling of concern for such people to keep him going. It is very difficult to maintain a concern for people who tell you to "get lost!" or who threaten to kill you if you do not relent. When you add to that the fact that entire populations often take this position—think, for instance of the so-called "closed" areas of the world—you will see that this work of Christ has always needed something more than concern for the lost to keep it moving ahead.

In the last analysis the only *sufficient* reason for evangelism is God. Michael Green, in his book *Evangelism in the Early Church*, wrote:

There can be little doubt that the main motive for evangelism was a theological one. These men did not spread their message because it was advisable for them to do so, nor because it was the socially responsible thing to do. They did not do it primarily for humanitarian or agathistic utilitarian reasons. They did it because of the overwhelming experience of the love of God which they had received through Jesus Christ.[2]

In writing this, Michael Green has come to the heart of Christian motivation. "The main motive...was a *theological* one." That is, it had to do, not with men and their needs but, with God. Let us look at this more closely.

It is God who sends us into the world. We would not deny the power exercised over the church by the awful need of the world, but at the end of the day, when we are weary and men and women have made it plain that they do not want us, we must fall back on the command of God. Christ has said, "Go!" In thinking on him we say with Thomas, "My Lord and my God!" (John 20:28). And then we go. If the world cares little or nothing for our witness, Christ cares a great deal for it. Just prior to ascending to heaven he promised the church his Holy Spirit and closely tied the Spirit's presence to our evangelism, an evangelism which would—as we now know—take centuries to accomplish. Listen:

> You will receive power when the Holy Spirit comes on you; and you will be my witnesses in Jerusalem, and in all Judea and Samaria, and to the ends of the earth (Acts 1:8).

What precisely is the nature of this connection between the Holy Spirit's coming and the spread of the gospel "to the ends of the earth?" The answer is complex, but one part of it is clear from elsewhere in the book of Acts. The Holy Spirit would grant them power to be obedient to their Lord's command. After Peter had told the leaders of Jerusalem that "we cannot help speaking about what we have seen and heard" (Acts 4:20), he joined his fellows in praying for boldness to do that very thing (Acts 4:29). The result? "After they prayed, the place where they were meeting was shaken. And they were all filled with the Holy Spirit and spoke the word of God boldly" (Acts 4:31). When Peter was later called on to defend their action he said simply, "We must obey God rather than men" (Acts 5:29).

God has spoken; that is sufficient. As Michael Green wrote, their reason was a theological one. Obedience to commands is not thought of very highly in our culture. Individual freedom has become for many the value against which all other values must be measured. But it was not always so. More importantly it will not be the measure by which we will be measured at Christ's return. The returning king will want to know what we have done with the goods with which he entrusted us. Perhaps he will remind us of his earlier words, "You are my friends if you do what I command" (John 15:14).

To be fully fair to Green, however, we must step back one step further in finding the motive for the early church's evangelism. When he spoke of their motive being a theological one, he was looking beyond their obedience to something that lay behind it, what Green called "a sense of gratitude." Man is a complex being. *You* are a complex being. You do not act from a single motive. Your life moves forward under the stimulus of many and varied impulses. Of these, one of the most powerful is gratitude.

It is possible for you to be obedient for more than one reason. If you cringe in fear as you go about your duties you are technically an obedient man, but your obedience will have very little to do with real Christianity. Slavish fear is no part of gospel motivation. Gratitude, on the other hand, lies very near the heart of it.

Someone may ask at this point, "Does the Bible not tell us we must fear God?" Yes, it does. But it is evident that *fear* in such contexts means to stand in awe of God. We must *fear* him in the sense of having reverence for him, a reverence that makes us take seriously both his promises and his commands. Then his goodness and greatness will move us to wonder and admiration, but that is a far cry from terror. "Perfect love," John tells us, "drives out [slavish] fear" (1 John 4:18).

In starting the second major section of his letter to Rome, Paul appealed to his readers to act out of gratitude for God's goodness to them: "Therefore I urge you, brothers, in view of God's mercy, to offer your bodies as living sacrifices, holy and pleasing to God— this is your spiritual act of worship" (Romans 12:1). This appeal is "in view of God's mercy." He might have written, "in view of God's judgment," but he did not. Later he reminded them that "we will all stand before God's judgment seat" (Romans 14:10). But at this pivotal point he chose the mercy of God as his rallying cry. A motive was wanted to move Christians to sacrificial living. Paul found that motive in gratitude to God.

Did Paul's Lord not teach us the same thing in Luke 7? There we read that Jesus went to eat at the home of a Pharisee named Simon. While they were at the table:

> a woman who had lived a sinful life...began to wet his feet with her tears. Then she wiped them them with her hair, kissed them and poured perfume on them (Luke 7:37–38).

This was a bit too much for the Pharisee who saw in it an evidence that Jesus was not a prophet. After all, a prophet would have known what kind of woman she was! What becomes clear, however, is this: Jesus knew both the woman and the Pharisee. So he made a comparison between them, a comparison based on the levels of their gratitude:

> "Do you see this woman [Jesus said]? You did not give me any water for my feet, but she wet my feet with her tears and wiped them with her hair. You did not give me a kiss, but this woman, from the time I entered, has not stopped kissing my feet. You did not put oil on my head, but she has poured perfume on my feet. Therefore, I tell you, her many sins have

been forgiven—for she loved much. But he who has been forgiven little loves little" (Luke 7:44–47).

Simon comes out poorly when compared with this "sinful woman." Why? Because gratitude moves men and women to go to heroic lengths in serving those to whom they are grateful. The lesson is not that the woman's great love led to the forgiveness of her sins. Not at all! Just the opposite was true. The forgiveness of her sins—which took place prior to Jesus telling her about it—led to her magnificent act of love. Simon, on the other hand, had no sins forgiven. As a result, he did not act like a man moved by gratitude.

What has all this to do with evangelism? A great deal! Gratitude for God's mercy does not confine itself to acts of love toward the physical body of Jesus. If it did, there would have been no such acts in the last 1,950 years. But gratitude is both *creative* and *responsive*. The sinful woman who dropped her tears on Jesus' feet had no command to do so. But she created acts of love to show her devotion to our Lord. The Romans, on the other hand, had the command of an inspired Apostle to respond to. And gratitude would lead them to yield their bodies as living sacrifices because it was the will of God.

We have the command of our Saviour to make disciples of all nations. A sense of gratitude for his many mercies to us will lead us to seek to carry out his command. It is clear that the command itself cannot be carried out by any individual. Therefore, it bears on us as individual Christian believers to do one part of it in concert with others. Our part may be small, but gratitude to God will move us to take that small part.

God's greatness is reason enough to do what he tells us to do, including evangelizing, preaching the gospel. But when we think that we who have been saved know the greatness of God primarily as *goodness*, then we cannot waver in our dedication to the task. We should not be slow to respond to the need of a dying world. But a great God, best known to us in a dying Saviour, has bound us to himself by cords of mercy. Can we say less than Isaiah said when he experienced the forgiving love of God? No, his words are our words, "Here am I. Send me!" (Isaiah 6:8).

14

ON THE ETHICS OF CONTROVERSY

It is the unhappy lot of any man who cares a fig for truth to be called on to engage in controversy. He may embrace it as a purse of gold or despise it as a putrefying sore, but he can no more escape it than he can escape the atmosphere or the common cold. In a fallen world, truth and controversy are bedfellows.

It is true: We cannot make progress by controversy alone. Real progress toward unity is the work of God. It is also true, however, that we are unlikely to make progress without controversy. All Scripture bears this out, not least when it couples the sovereignty of God with the use of means in the highest interests of the soul. We do not simply hope for the day in which all will be absolutely in one accord. No, we seek *by means* to bring "every thought captive to the obedience of Christ" (2 Corinthians 10:5). A man may spend valuable time bemoaning the fact, but what is needed is a way to come to terms with it as a godly man, a way to carry on controversy with a minimum amount of damage to his opponent and to the

This essay first appeared in *Reformation & Revival Journal*, 5, No. 4 (Fall 1996), 147–158.

interested bystander and the maximum amount of good to the cause of God and truth.

But how to do it?—That is the question. How shall we carry on the controversies that have been laid upon us by the providence of God? Let me propose a few rules for guidance in the minefield of vigorous controversy, especially among those who profess faith in our common Lord Jesus.

SHOW RESPECT FOR THE PERSONS WITH WHOM YOU DIFFER

In an article entitled "The Scope and Center of Old Testament Theology and Hope," Kenneth Barker lays down a number of points that are crucial to his theme. For example as his fifth point he writes, *"To say that the Old Testament is the testament of law but the New Testament is the testament of grace is a false dichotomy."* Both his stated subject and this fifth point show that his interest is biblical and theological. The surprising thing, however, is his first point in this biblical and theological discussion. Here Barker writes: *"Dispensational premillenialists and amillenial, covenant theologians of orthodox persuasion should treat each other more like brothers in Christ and less like adversaries or even heretics."*[1]

Clearly this plea by Barker is off the subject—or is it? The very fact that he thought it needed saying as a major point in a biblical and theological discussion is a sad commentary on the state of controversy among Evangelicals in the early twenty-first century.[2] If we respect the persons of even those who have committed capital crimes as they await execution because they are men made in the image of God,[3] how much more must we respect the persons of those who oppose us from within the Christian camp? We are commanded to love those who belong to Christ. Can we then treat them with less than fullest consideration?

GIVE YOUR OPPONENT
ACCURATE DEFINITIONS OF YOUR KEY IDEAS

Nearly everyone has made the observation that controversy often is rooted in misunderstanding. This conviction grows with maturity as we experience how difficult the art of communication really is. To say what you mean and to hear what the other person means are often beyond our capacities. We are finite creatures; worse, we are sinful creatures. Both of these facts work against our making ourselves clear. Our finitude makes it difficult for us to clearly grasp our own ideas, so as to define them accurately. Our sinfulness adds to the difficulty by making us impatient with those who "pretend" not to understand us. Yet definition is vital. As Bishop J.C. Ryle once wrote: "It may be laid down as a rule, with tolerable confidence, that the absence of accurate definitions is the very life of religious controversy. If men would only define with precision the theological terms which they use, many disputes would die."[4] Can we doubt that he was right?

WHEN IN DOUBT, PUT AN ORTHODOX CONSTRUCTION ON YOUR OPPONENT'S WORDS

With the best will in the world, this will not always be possible. The critical words here are "when in doubt." Another widespread observation is as follows: If you think about what another has said, you may often realize that it is not objectional after all. To put it another way, our first impressions of others' language, like our first impression of others' persons, is often inaccurate. Some examples may help.

Would you subscribe to the statement, "The Bible *contains* the Word of God"? Evangelicals who might otherwise use that language have generally abandoned it. Why? Because to many who hear it, it asserts an old liberal thesis: The Bible contains the Word of God along with a larger or smaller mixture of human error. Yet the statement is unobjectionable when understood in another way: The Bible contains the Word of God without remainder. Those of us who believe in inerrancy could raise no reasonable objection to that.

Or how about this statement, "Jesus Christ was a man." Taken in a certain context this might mean, "Jesus Christ was a man and nothing more or less." No Christian theologian could countenance such an understanding for a moment. Jesus Christ is the God-man, truly and fully human, yet truly and fully divine in the profoundest sense. In a context, however, that demanded a statement of the full humanity of Christ, "Jesus Christ was a man," is the proper assertion without any stated qualification whatever.

NEVER ATTRIBUTE TO YOUR OPPONENT MORE THAN HE ASSERTS

It is so easy, because we think we see where his statement is bound to take him, to decide that he has already come to these apparently logical conclusions. You know the kind of thing we say: "If he believes A then he must believe B and C also." But we must sternly discipline ourselves to avoid drawing conclusions about what our opponent *must* believe. This point has been put forcefully by Andrew Fuller, the nineteenth-century Baptist theologian:

> [P]rinciples and their consequences are so suddenly associated in the mind, that when we hear a person avow the former, we can scarcely forbear immediately attributing to him the latter. If a principle be proposed to us *for acceptance*, it is right to weigh the consequences; but when forming our judgment of the person who holds it, we should attach nothing to him but what he perceives and avows.[5]

In my judgment, we have done an enormous amount of injustice to others by failing to keep this in mind.

It is far better to react as Jonathan Edwards did in writing about the book of a certain "Mr. W."

> [W]hen I take notice of these things in his book, my aim is not to beget in you an ill opinion of Mr. W as though he were as corrupt in his settled persuasion, as one would be ready to think...if it should be supposed, that he embraced all the *consequences* of what he here maintains. Men often do not see or allow the plain consequences of their own doctrines. And therefore, though I charge very pernicious consequences on some *things* he says, yet I do not charge *him* with embracing these consequences...[6]

Both logic and love dictate this kind of response from us.

SUSPECT A MAN'S JUDGMENT
BEFORE YOU SUSPECT HIS SINCERITY

The reason for this is clear. To have unclear judgment is an intellectual problem to which no guilt necessarily attaches (though it may). But to distrust someone's sincerity is to strike at the heart of his or her moral character. Yet nothing is more common in controversy than for opponents to disparage each other's integrity. This is a sin against charity at the very least, unless the grounds upon which it is done are beyond question.

It is no small thing, of course, to throw doubt on a man's ability to reason—it should never be done lightly. But that is often what honest controversy is about. Our errors of logic are frequent and "very pernicious," to borrow Jonathan Edwards' phrase in the quotation above. We do one another a loving service when we are able to point out such fallacies.

BE READY TO BELIEVE THAT THE TRUTH
IS LARGER THAN YOU HAVE UNDERSTOOD IT TO BE

Like many men, I abounded in self-confidence when I was young. For me everything was, as we like to say, "black or white." To admit that some areas might be *gray* seemed to be a betrayal of truth. After all, if A was true, then its opposite, B, was bound to be false, and that was that!

No, I have not abandoned the logic of the previous sentence; it is irrational to do so. Unlike some of my contemporaries I have no desire to defend irrationalism. But I would like to defend modesty, not simply as a grace in itself but as a means of learning also. Somewhere years ago I ran across the following statement: "You are more likely to be right in what you assert than in what you deny." Statistically I do not know whether the author of that statement was right or wrong, but eventually it opened up a new world to my pinched powers of reason. It brought me to the conviction that heads this section. The truth on any subject is likely to be larger than I had imagined it could be.

The determination not to learn from others often accompanies the certainty that we are right. That is unfortunate; one might almost say insidious. Take the matter of the natures of the Lord Jesus. To say "Jesus is a man," suggests to almost any biblically uninformed mind that Jesus is *not* God. Nor is that impulse entirely evil. To say "Tom Wells is a man," leads to the same impulse. It is predicated on the idea, which proves to be false in one case only, that man and God are two entirely distinct categories. Man is one thing, a created thing, and God is another, the Creator in fact. This, of course, is just an illustration, though true in itself. I have chosen it because it is not likely to be denied by Christians, but the obvious supernatural quality of the person of Jesus Christ is unlike the kinds of truths that we are likely to find when keeping my maxim in mind. So let us take another example.

I belong to a small, doctrinally precise movement within Reformed circles. *We have the truth.* The preceding sentence is written only partially tongue-in-cheek; it is our honest conviction. More than that, when looked at as a system, this truth sets us apart from most Evangelicals. It has some hard edges and sharp corners that are not acceptable to the evangelical culture. Nevertheless, we are not prepared to give them up. This would seem to mean that other Evangelicals need us desperately, given the divergence of our views, but we do not have much need of them. We are right; they are wrong.

This analysis, however, runs into a serious problem with Scripture. The problem is not that they are right and we are wrong. Even if that were true (which of course it cannot be!) that would only put the shoe on the other foot, not really changing the situation, but only changing the players. No, the problem is much bigger than that.

The problem is this: The Scripture teaches that every Christian needs every other Christian, and it is not right to minimize and marginalize that need. We need one another because that is the way the Holy Spirit has "constructed" the body of Christ. Paul is adamant about this.

But now there are many members, but one body. And the eye cannot say to the hand, "I have no need of you"; or again the head to the feet, "I have no need of you." On the contrary, it is much truer that the members of the body which seem to be weaker are necessary (1 Corinthians 12:20–22).

In this quotation I have simply sampled what Paul has to say on this subject, but I selected enough to show two vital truths. First, every Christian needs every other; second, effort to confine that need to relatively unimportant matters is impossible.[7]

Let us see if we can make this concrete, by trying to lay out two opposite positions on the spectrum of genuine faith in Christ. For the sake of illustration we will put my own position, Calvinistic Baptist, over against the Pentecostal position. Since we vary on a large number of issues, it is easy for me to see how they need people of my persuasion, but it is hard to see what we need from them. (And they, no doubt, have the same problem!) What shall we do?

There is one easy solution. I can write them off by saying they are not Christians. (You may have noticed that I begged an important question in the last paragraph when I spoke of "genuine faith in Christ." How do I know that their faith is "genuine?") I have friends who have taken this path.[8]

But there is another possibility, the possibility that they have things to teach me or comfort to give me or rebuke to bring to me that I cannot yet envision. In other words, the truth connected with faith in Jesus Christ may be larger and more wonderful than I (and they) have ever imagined. To try to illustrate what "I have never imagined" is, of course, beyond me. I must be content to see how this works out in the providence of God, and I feel certain that it will.

CONCLUSIONS

First, some conclusions that we must *not* draw:

1) We must not conclude that in order to be ethical in conducting controversy we have to recognize men as Christians when they

fail the biblical tests of Christianity. As Donald Carson has written (applying to our contemporary scene a truth earlier espoused by J. Gresham Machen):

> At some point one must face the fact that the kinds of disavowals and denials one finds in many branches of classic liberalism, and repeated by the major proponents of religious pluralism, are much deeper even than the chasms between, say, Russian Orthodoxy and American Pentecostalism, or between Roman Catholicism and classic evangelicalism; we are dealing with "different religions," in the strongest sense of that expression.[9]

2) We must not conclude that it is wrong to press the points on which we feel confident. To adopt this position would be to paralyze all discussion. It would stop us from loving others and seeking their good by correcting them where they need correction. And, incidentally but viciously, if others adopted the same position toward us we would lose the help their criticism offers. As Andrew Fuller has written:

> If we wish to know the truth, we must read those who think differently from us, who, whether they be impartial towards us or not, will be much more likely to detect our faults than we are to detect them ourselves.[10]

On the contrary we must contend for what we hold to be truth.

> [T]o proceed with a healthy doubt about one's own moral rightness only means treating one's opponents with respect and granting the possibility of error. It does not mean refraining from action. The legal scholar Michael Perry, himself a Roman Catholic, has put the point nicely: "Although we must resist infallibilism…at any given moment our convictions are what they are."[11]

If we do not act on such convictions, how will truth make its way in this world?

3) Closely related to the two previous points, we must not conclude that it is wrong to vigorously denounce critical error. The example of our Lord Jesus and the apostles shows this plainly. Though they spoke by inspiration and we do not, yet passionate regard for truth will move us to speak and write with a zeal commensurate with the importance of the error with which we are dealing *after* we have exhausted all avenues that might show that we have misunderstood what has been said. We must never forget: Some errors are damning.

Let me add some positive conclusions:

1) Given the importance of controversy, we must not avoid it out of cowardice. No one likes to lose friends or be scorned unnecessarily, but there is only one person who commands our absolute allegiance: God, as he has revealed himself in his written and personal Word. Faithfulness to him has always occasioned controversy and it always will.

2) Controversy is to be done as gently and compassionately as is consistent with zeal for the truth. In the words of J.I. Packer:

> There are good and bad ways of fulfilling the ministry of criticism among Christians. This ministry is important, for all who seek truth and wisdom take up from time to time with wrong ideas and need correction. But discussion and debate ordinarily achieve more than gestures of denunciation. To think of sustained denunciation as the essence of faithful witness…is very wrong. Denouncing error has its place, but since it easily appears arrogant and generates much unfruitful unhappiness, anyone who feels drawn to it should take a lot of advice before yielding to the urge.[12]

Donald Carson has made the same point in speaking of Francis Schaeffer.

> One of the reasons for Francis Schaeffer's influence was his ability to present his analysis of the culture with a tear in his eye. Whether or not one agrees at every point with his analysis, and regardless of how severe his judgments were, one could not responsibly doubt his compassion, his genuine love for men and women. Too many of his would-be successors simply sound like angry people. Our times call for Christian leaders who will articulate the truth boldly, courageously, humbly, knowledgeably, in a contemporary fashion—and with profound compassion. One cannot imagine how the kind of gospel set forth in the Bible could be effectively communicated in any other way... [We] serve the One who, on seeing large crowds, "had compassion on them, because they were like sheep without a shepherd" (Mark 6:34; cf. Matthew 9:36).[13]

If these words describe accurately, as they do, the gentleness and compassion that we must use toward those who do not know our Saviour, how much more must we adopt such attitudes toward brothers and sisters in Christ?

I found the following admonition strikingly set out as poetry.

Controversy in religion is a hateful thing.
It is hard enough to fight the devil,
the world, and the flesh,
without private differences in our
own camp ———
But there is one thing
which is even worse than controversy,
and that is false doctrine tolerated,
allowed, and permitted without
protest or molestation ...
Three things there are which men

never ought to trifle with:
 a little poison,
 a little false doctrine,
 and a little sin.[14]

Spirituality

15

THE SOURCES
OF OUR SANCTIFICATION

The word *piety*, if I understand it correctly, refers to the devout attitudes and feelings that a Christian believer must have and cultivate toward God the Father, Christ the Son and the Holy Spirit. It is a fair reading of Scripture to say that the new birth brings such attitudes and feelings with it. Every Christian may truly say, "I love him because he first loved me." Without such love Christianity in an individual is but a shell of the real thing. Piety accompanies the first breaths of the Christian life as the new believer is born into the family of God.

Piety, however, must also be cultivated. As with all else that the Father works within the believer at the outset of his or her Christian life, there is a process of growth and development that must follow the initial gift. The goal is to be like the Lord Jesus in all one's moral character. The process that targets this goal is called by theologians *sanctification*. Hence, the title of this essay, "The sources of our sanctification." If we must be sanctified, how shall we go about it? Or, alternately, how shall God work this conformity to his Son within our daily lives?

This question came home to me recently in reading a book entitled *The Weakness of the Law*.[1] The book is further defined as a "timely defense of the third use of the law," as set forth by the leaders of the Reformation and especially John Calvin. In brief the *third use* was the usefulness of the moral law in promoting the sanctification of the believer. In the author's words, "The first two uses are the condemnation of unrighteousness in the sinner, and the social role of restraining those who are particularly unruly. The 'third use' refers to the function of the moral law as the pattern of life for the believer." The moral law (or the Ten Commandments), in this view "exercises a key role in sanctification when employed by the Holy Spirit..."[2] From the days of the Reformation, then, until the present hour, Bible students have sought to pinpoint the sources of the believer's sanctification. What tools does God use, and what tools does he put into the hands of his people, to promote the various facets of their sanctification, including the growth of piety? The question is just as pressing today as it was at any time in history.

THE GOAL OF THE CHRISTIAN LIFE

We start with documenting from Scripture the goal of the Christian life. Paul describes it in these words, "For those whom he foreknew he also predestined to be conformed to the image of his Son, in order that he [the Son] might be the firstborn within a large family" (Romans 8:29). Here Paul puts it plainly: The goal of the Christian life is to be made like the Lord Jesus. This will include, of course, other things besides conformity to the moral character of the Lord Jesus, for example, a glorified body. But no doubt a major part of this goal is moral and spiritual change. God has made us his sons, as Jesus is his Son, so that we would bear the family likeness. That lies on the face of the passage.

We need to know something more than the goal, however. We need to see that we reach it by a process. That is, God does not wait till our deaths to work this renovation in us. Instead, he works on it day and night in our lives. Two more statements by Paul bear this out. Speaking to believers at Philippi, Paul says, "[I]t is God who is at work in you, enabling you both to will and to work for his good pleasure" (Philippians 2:13). To the Corinthians he writes, "And all of us [Christians], with unveiled faces, seeing the glory of the Lord as though reflected in a mirror, are being transformed into the same image from one degree of glory to another; for this comes from the Lord, the Spirit" (2 Corinthians 3:18). The work of God in the Christian goes on throughout the Christian life, making the believer more like the Lord Jesus little by little. So sanctification is a life-long process. Our question again is, What does God use in our lives to continue approaching the goal of likeness to Christ?

To discuss the sources of our sanctification I would like to move from the general to the particular. I will start with an all-embracing answer before we look more closely at the details.

AN ALL-EMBRACING SOURCE OF SANCTIFICATION

The all-embracing answer to this question is found in reflecting on both Romans 8:28 and 8:29. Here they are together:

> We know that all things work together for good for those who love God, who are called according to his purpose. For those whom he foreknew he also predestined to be conformed to the image of his Son, in order the he might be the firstborn within a large family.

Let me make several points here. First, you will see that while the order of the verses obscures it slightly, verse 28 is a conclusion based upon the truth in verse 29. Paul's argument goes like this: Since God has predestined believers to be like Jesus, he has put a plan into place that will foster that goal. The plan is this: God will make everything the Christian experiences work for the believer's "good." If we ask what that "good" is, the context defines it as being like the Lord Jesus.

Second, our Christian experience bears this out by eliminating many other "goods" that might first occur to us when we read these verses. Let us name some of them, starting with *health*. Do all things we experience work together to give us good health? We might wish it were so, but it is not. Some of God's choicest saints have borne the burden of ill health through most of their lives. Romans 8:28 certainly does not promise us good health. Or take *prosperity*. Other things being equal (they never are, of course!), to prosper economically is a great good. But it is not the good promised in this passage. If Paul meant that prosperity was what God works for all his people, Paul's own life would have proved the idea false. Here is his testimony: "I know what it is to have little, and I know what it is to have plenty. In any and all circumstances I have learned the secret of being well-fed and of going hungry, of having plenty and of being in need" (Philippians 4:12). Paul actually knew very little of prosperity after he came to Christ. Instead he knew want and suffering. That was no accident. The Lord told Ananias about Paul, "I myself will show him how much he must suffer for the sake of my name" (Acts 9:16). And suffer he did! We could continue on through various other "goods" that God has not promised, but it is unnecessary. In each case we would get the same result.

The third point is the critical one for our discussion. Romans 8:28 tells us in no uncertain terms that God uses everything that happens to us to further our sanctification. The first source, then, is all-embracing. No wonder that "we are more than conquerors through him who loved us" (Romans 8:37)! What can defeat the Christian, if his every experience does him good by making him more like Christ? Our first answer to the question of the sources of our sanctification is a glorious one. It is full of encouragement and help for the weakest believer.

ANOTHER SOMEWHAT COMPREHENSIVE ANSWER

The second source of our sanctification is probably the one most Christians think of first, the Bible, the Word of God. Many of us are immediately propelled toward this answer by remembering the request of the Lord Jesus. Praying to his Father he said, "Sanctify them through thy truth; thy word is truth" (John 17:17). The thought in this verse, however, is somewhat narrower than the sanctification of believers everywhere and at all times. Here sanctification refers to the original followers of Christ in their mission to the world. (The transition to all believers comes in verse 20 where Jesus extends his prayer: "I ask not only on behalf of these, but also on behalf of those who will believe in me through their word…") But the sanctification of the apostles to their task entailed godly living, like Jesus' own, as a means to the conversion of others. This is already implied in the promise of persecution for the sake of Jesus (John 15:18–25). It is put beyond all doubt, however, by Jesus' words, "I give you a new commandment that you love one another…By this everyone will know that you are my disciples, if you have love for one another" (John 13:34–35). So in principle their sanctification to service was not all that different from our own. We too are sent into the world, and we too must follow this command and cherish its promise. And when we are taught to "Pursue peace with everyone, and the holiness [sanctification] without which no one will see the Lord" (Hebrews 12:14), we discover that sanctification is our responsibility. No evangelical Christian will doubt that our main resource must be the inerrant Word of God. The only question that we must answer is this: What portion(s) of God's Word will best serve to make us like the Lord Jesus? And here, historically, the debate suddenly becomes hot and heavy!

TWO HISTORICAL ANSWERS

Earlier I mentioned the book *The Weakness of the Law*. One valuable feature of it is a survey of what has been called the Antinomian controversy in the English-speaking world. Starting with the Puritans in the sixteenth century and running right into our own day, Jonathan Bayes describes this debate:

> The point at issue may be summarized as follows: Does the moral element in the law of the Old Testament continue to have binding force and directing power in the life of the

believer, such that it exercises a key role in sanctification when employed by the Holy Spirit, or does the Holy Spirit work directly, or, if He employs any means at all, is the Gospel of justification by grace through faith in Christ the sole and sufficient instrument of sanctification? This latter position has been called "doctrinal antinomianism", and it must be distinguished from "practical antinomianism". The issue is not whether Christians ought in practice to keep the law but whether the law is itself a means to this end.[3]

I have quoted Bayes at length to show some of the options Christians have adopted over the centuries.

1) Some Christians have said that the Bible is not a source of sanctification at all, since the Holy Spirit creates sanctification directly, without using means.
2) Other have said that the Spirit uses the gospel alone to promote sanctification.
3) Still others have given a key role to the moral law (often equated with the Ten Commandments) in producing sanctification.

Who is right, here? It seems clear to me that all three are right, except when they eliminate each others' positions. There seems to be no need to make a choice here. Remembering again the all-embracing promise of Romans 8:28 should help us to see that truth. In fact, this seems so plain that it is hard to understand why there was controversy over it. Why did the problem not simply disappear as time went on? The answer is complex, but I will try to throw a little light on it.

First, it is obvious that the question of sanctification, like all theological questions, is involved closely with conclusions we draw on other theological issues. All reasoning is done from presuppositions. That is true in the case of the Bible. Once we think we know the meaning of an individual verse, we bring that meaning to the next verse we examine and presuppose that the second verse cannot contradict the first. (I am describing, of course, the reasoning of those who believe in the full inspiration of Scripture. Others may not be put off by supposed contradictions.) In this way, each previous verse controls what we see in the next one we look at. Where that does not happen, our understanding of the latest verse may require a revision in our understanding of a previous verse or verses. In any case, while we hopefully never cease learning from Scripture, before too long we come to hold a rudimentary "systematic theology" based on our study. When we add to this mixture the opinions about Scripture and theology that we have absorbed from others, we wind up with a fairly rich brew that we call "our convictions." (And may heaven help the man or woman who contradicts them!)

The point here is that "scholars" are not at all exempt from this process. The difference is that, by sheer dint of study, they eventually come to an enormous number of such convictions. Those convictions soon turn up in the form of commentaries on Scripture and the formal systematic theologies and creeds that become part of the heritage of each generation of Christians. The process is inevitable, and it is not essentially evil. We may describe it as "very good" even, as long as we realize that it is never perfect. Now let me try to apply what we have just seen to these variations on the sources of sanctification.

One important doctrine strongly emphasized at the Reformation was the doctrine of justification by faith. Closely related to this, and destined to bring enormous difficulties in its wake, was the doctrine of the role of works in men's lives. That led to a problem. The strong emphasis on justification by faith alone produced a de-emphasis on works in the minds of many. In some important respects this was a healthy reaction to earlier distortion in the Roman church. But, trying to balance these two ideas, justification by faith and the necessity of good works, men came to differing opinions. Some thought that the best way to guard against works-righteousness was to deny that Christians should apply themselves to righteous actions. This group was later represented in those who held position one (1) above. They agreed that Christians should produce righteous works, but thought that the Holy Spirit would see that it was done without human means. Others thought that the motivating power of the glorious gospel message would ensure that Christians would act righteously (as far as that was possible in a fallen world). This group was later represented by position two (2) above. Finally, many thought that preaching moral law was the best guarantee that Christians would live righteous lives. This group was later represented by those who held position three (3) above. In Bayes' study, this would be the typical Puritans of the seventeenth century. Of the three groups, this last group did not deny either the direct work of the Spirit or the profitableness of the gospel in promoting sanctification.

For many, these facts have made the Puritans the best models for promoting sanctification among Christians today. Indeed, if we had to choose between the three groups, given the Puritans' openness to the other views, we would have to take them as our exemplars. But there is more to be said.

In my judgment, there is nothing in Scripture that warrants *the amount* of emphasis the Puritans put upon moral law as a means of sanctification. (This is especially true when moral law is simply identified with the Decalogue as was common among the Puritans.) I have tried to show already that Romans 8:28 makes it very doubtful whether any one thing should be looked on as the preeminent means God uses. That does, of course, leave open the question that remains important to us: Granting the direct work of the Spirit, what must *we* emphasize in our preaching and teaching from the Word of God?

This is a tough question to give an exact answer to, but we can approach the answer best, perhaps, by making a few observations. First, we must emphasize that the ethic of the New Testament goes well beyond any fair reading of the Ten Commandments.[4] It is sometimes argued that the fuller revelation in the Law of Christ is *implicit* in the Decalogue. It is hard either to defend or to deny this idea owing to the ambiguity of the word implicit. But at the very least we must say that the New Testament extends the literal meaning of the Decalogue enormously. Even the rest of the Old Testament moves beyond the Ten Commandments in its increasing emphasis on inwardness as Israel drifts farther and farther from God and the doctrine of *the remnant* develops.

That said, a strong case can be made for large doses of both the law of Christ and the gospel of Christ, two sides of the same coin, as concurrent promoters of sanctification. The reason is apparent: Christ's law shows the direction in which we must head, and his gospel keeps us from the weariness that leads ultimately to losing heart in the battle against sin. That is why the writer to the Hebrews exhorted his readers both to "pursue holiness" (Hebrews 12:14) and to do it by

> looking to Jesus the pioneer and perfecter of our faith, who for the sake of the joy that was set before him endured the cross, disregarding its shame, and has taken his seat at the right hand of the throne of God. Consider him who endured such hostility against himself from sinners, so that you may not grow weary or lose heart (Hebrews 12:2–3).

These words are our instructions. To "pursue" sanctification we must fix our attention on Jesus (compare "looking to" him in verse 2 and "Consider him" in verse 3). In fulfilling the Torah (Mosaic Law), Jesus Christ has become the object of our affections and the Master of our lives. In his example, in his teaching and in the teaching of his agents, his apostles and prophets, we have the instruction and ethic that we need for this present age. His church is "built upon the foundation of the apostles and prophets, with Christ Jesus himself as the cornerstone" (Ephesians 2:20).[5]

WHAT ELSE BESIDES THE SCRIPTURES?

If we accept the work of the Spirit and the Word of God as the chief sources of our sanctification, are there other things referred to in Romans 8:28 that are important enough to mention individually. Let me suggest several.

One source of our sanctification with great potential for good is the prayers of others. This will, of course, include the intercession of Christ and the Spirit (Romans 8:26–27,34), but I am thinking here of the prayers of other believers in Christ. The New Testament demonstrates this by the zeal with which the early church engaged in prayer for one another and also by the requests for prayer that dot its pages. In Acts 12 Peter is in prison, guarded day and night. But "[w]hile Peter was kept in prison, the church prayed fervently to God for him" (Acts 12:5). Not only were their prayers answered, but Peter's faith was increased. At first he thought his release was a vision (Acts 12:9), but shortly he realized that the Lord had specially blessed him. "Then Peter came to himself and said, 'Now I am sure that the Lord has sent his angel and rescued me from the hands of Herod and all that the Jewish people were expecting'" (Acts 12:11).

Paul often mentions his prayers for others, including their sanctification. To the Philippians he writes,

> And this is my prayer, that your love may overflow more and more with knowledge and full insight to help you to determine what is best, so that in the day of Christ you may be pure and blameless, having produced the harvest of righteousness that comes through Jesus Christ for the glory and praise of God (Philippians 1:9–11).

Note in these verses how Paul looks both at the process of sanctification and its ultimate goal. He prays for those things that will help them "to determine what is best." Then he looks ahead to the day of Christ in which they will be found "pure and blameless" and "having produced the harvest of righteousness." More than that, he asks others to pray for him and other saints:

> [A]lways persevere in supplication for all the saints. Pray also for me, so that when I speak, a message may be given to me to make known with boldness the mystery of the gospel, for which I am an ambassador in chains. Pray that I may declare it boldly, as I must speak (Ephesians 6:18–20).

Paul was a man under orders. His sanctification included faithfulness to his Lord in preaching the gospel.

We must never forget that the model prayer that our Lord gave us teaches us to ask its petitions for our brothers and sisters as well as ourselves. The language is "Give *us* this day *our* daily bread. And forgive *us our* debts as *we* also have forgiven *our* debtors. And do not bring *us* to the time of trial, but rescue *us* from the evil one." Such requests as these promote the sanctification of our fellow believers.

Then, in history much has been said about the *sacraments* as sources of sanctification. The idea that has come to be associated with the word sacrament is the idea of a sacred sign or symbol that in one way or another conveys grace (gracious help from God) to the person who receives it. The Roman Catholic church identifies seven different acts as sacraments that are alleged to have been instituted by the Lord Jesus. Protestants, on the other hand, confine the word to two things, baptism and the Lord's Supper. Some use the word *ordinances*, things ordained by the Lord Jesus, instead of the word sacraments.

Do the sacraments or ordinances convey to believers God's gracious help toward sanctification? A cautious yes seems to be the answer. The caution arises from the physical and material character of these actions. Physical actions and materials may enter our eyes, fall on our ears, or even enter our digestive systems with no spiritual effect whatsoever. So there can be nothing automatic about seeing or participating in either baptism or the Lord's Supper.

The yes arises from the assumption that participants in the sacraments or ordinances know what these acts are about. When that is the case, they function very much like the Word of God does. They convey truth. They are like visible words from God that convey to both participants and onlookers encouraging facts about our relation to Christ in his death and resurrection. Such facts, whether spoken or seen, promote love to God and gratitude to him for his grace among true believers.[6]

When we make progress in our Christian lives, we are said to be progressing in sanctification. That raises the question, Do we then also grow in piety, the devout attitudes and feelings that a Christian believer wishes to cultivate toward the triune God? Or is it possible for a true believer in Christ to fall into a barren intellectualism devoid of love to God?

The answers to these questions are not as simple as they may first seem. Several things complicate them. First is the question of each believer's native temperament, which reacts both on themselves and others. Some are optimistic, others pessimistic. The question, Do I love the Lord? may haunt some who very much love him. In this case, the judgment of others should be brought to bear on the question. On the other hand, another person may confidently boast of loving God and Christ, when others might well question their love.

Beyond that, we must think of what characterizes us and others. A Christian may suffer a season of barren spiritual feelings. But one swallow is not a summer, and one bout with lack of warmth in feelings is not apostasy. Again, it is what characterizes us that is the important measure of our spiritual lives.

Finally, if piety is an attitude of love toward God, and it is, we must know what love is. Is love an attitude or feeling of affection? Yes, it is; but it is not just any feeling of affection, however strong. It is an attitude or feeling of affection that leads us to seek the benefit of, or promote the interest of, another—in this case, God. Feelings or attitudes that do not move us to advance the program of God by obedience to his Word are delusive. On the other hand, where there is an earnest desire to obey God for God's own sake, we love him indeed. You need not take my word for it; here are the words of the Lord Jesus: "They who have my commandments and keep them are those who love me; and those who love me will be loved by my Father, and I will love them and reveal myself to them" (John 14:21).

Take heart!

16

THE HOLINESS OF GOD AND
THE ASSURANCE THAT I AM A CHRISTIAN

It is no easy matter to define the holiness of God. In this chapter we narrowly confine ourselves to a single observation about God's holiness: God's holiness demands a corresponding holiness and righteousness in us. God himself has plainly commanded: "I am the Lord your God. Consecrate yourselves therefore, and be holy; for I am holy" (Leviticus 11:44). This, of course, was spoken to his ancient people, Israel, but when we turn to the New Testament we hear it repeated to the church of Jesus Christ:

> As obedient children, do not be conformed to the former lusts which were yours in your ignorance, but like the Holy One who called you, be holy yourselves also in all your behavior; because it is written, "You shall be Holy, for I am Holy" (1 Peter 1:14–16).

In other words, we are to be like God. We are to be like God in

This essay first appeared in *Reformation & Revival Journal*, 4, No. 2 (Spring 1995), 63–71.

our moral character. Nor is this pious advice to be taken or left aside as the moment dictates. This is basic to the entire Christian life. If we are not holy we will never "see the Lord" (Hebrews 12:14). In the boldest of terms, "It is holiness or hell."

But I find all this quite intolerable. It is not that it causes me intellectual problems as though it were somehow irrational for God to call on me to be holy. The command itself makes sense, but I have a problem of another kind. I am unholy, and try as I may I cannot convince myself that I shall ever measure up to this simple standard—the holiness of God. Certainly I fall far short just now.

How then can I be a Christian? I have examined myself to see whether I am in the faith (as 2 Corinthians 13:5 exhorts me), and I find that I can give no certain answer. I have sought to take seriously Peter's command to make my calling and election sure (2 Peter 1:10), but doubt, based on uncertainty about the worthiness of my walk, dogs my footsteps and nudges me toward despair. I repeat, this time with still further apprehension: "How then can I be a Christian?"

In the previous two paragraphs I have cast the experience of many Christians in the first person to bring it vividly before our minds. For such men and women, the holiness of God that is to be reproduced in their lives stands like a roadblock on the way to a settled assurance. They can see no way around it. Perhaps you find yourself in this predicament; perhaps you have a friend afflicted in this way. Is there help? I think there is.

We must discard at once the answer of cheap grace, as in the following quip from Heinrich Heppe: "Things are admirably arranged. God likes forgiving sins, and I like committing them." In this scenario there is no concern at all for personal holiness. No, we must seek an answer to the question of personal assurance that comes to grips with the absolute necessity of conforming to the law of God. Yet, oddly enough, unless you have robust assurance already, it is well in most cases to temporarily set to one side the demand for personal holiness. Let me show you why this is so by discussing the book that, above all others, speaks to us about the tests of Christian reality—the Epistle of 1 John.

HISTORICAL CONTEXT OF 1 JOHN

1 John, like all the books of the New Testament, arises out of a distinct historical situation. The writer, John, found himself faced with the apostasy of some for whom he once had entertained great hope. But these "brethren" proved false. They forsook John, Christ's special messenger, and in that way they forsook Christ himself. As John wrote: "He who knows God listens to us; he who is not from God does not listen to us. By this we know the spirit of truth and the spirit of error" (1 John 4:6). John could speak in this authoritative way, not because he was proud, but because he had been specially sent by Christ himself to give the church inspired revelation.

But when these men forsook John they did not give up the claim to being Christians. As John writes his letter he speaks to others who apparently were remaining true to the Lord Jesus. Here, then, is the salient point: John constantly has the other men in his mind, the unfaithful men who yet claimed to know Jesus Christ. Much of what we read in his epistle is shaped by this fact. And this is especially the case when John sets down the thing that characterizes the letter as a whole: The tests that determine the truth or falsity of a man's profession of faith.

How does this affect what John writes? This means that generally speaking John's tests are for those who profess robust faith in Jesus Christ. Since I think this point has often been overlooked, it bears repeating. John is setting forth tests of Christianity *primarily* for men or women who are *confident that they belong to Christ*. If we miss this presupposition on John's part, I believe that we will also miss much of the point of what he has written. He is not thinking, in the first instance, of a poor trembling soul seeking to know whether or not he is saved. Rather he has in his mind's eye the man or woman who says, "I know Christ, and nothing you can say will make me doubt it." His tests may be useful to others as we will yet see, but they were originally set forth to examine the claims of those who did not doubt that they were true Christians. That does not mean that John was still assessing the state of those who had forsaken him and his Lord. He had already taken their measure.

No, he was writing for the church of his day and for us, but he was doing it from the standpoint of one who saw the necessity for testing even the most confident faith. In this way two things could be accomplished: some would be confirmed in their assurance that they belonged to Christ; others could begin to call their own confidence into question, either to have it confirmed later or to see themselves exposed as false disciples.

THREE TESTS FOR GENUINE CHRISTIANITY

John tests the Christian faith of his readers in three main ways:

1) He shows them that they must hold orthodox views of Christ if they are to consider themselves Christians. For example, there was a doctrine in the air in those days that separated the human Jesus from the divine Christ. To this John responded, "Who is the liar but the one who denies that Jesus is the Christ?" (1 John 2:22). To be a liar in John's view excluded one from being a Christian.

2) He makes plain that those who live ungodly lives cannot be Christians. "Little children," he writes, "let no one deceive you; the one who practices righteousness is righteous, just as He is righteous; the one who practices sin is of the Devil" (1 John 3:7–8).

3) He lays down love of the brethren as an acid test of Christian faith. "We know we have passed out of death into life, because we love the brethren. He who does not love abides in death" (1 John 3:14). This is, of course, not a mere profession of love that we must have. It is the self-sacrificial spirit found in our Lord Jesus. "We know love by this, that He laid down His life for us; and we ought to lay down our lives for the brethren. But whoever has the world's goods, and beholds his brother in need and closes his heart against him, how does the love of God abide in him?" (1 John 3:16–17). Clearly the man whose "love" is not evident in readiness for sacrificial giving deceives himself about being a Christian.

We may summarize these three tests as the tests of (1) orthodoxy, (2) godliness and (3) love.

For the purposes of this chapter we are concerned primarily with the second and third tests, godliness and love. In these two tests we confront the holiness of God where it impinges on our own thoughts, words and deeds. In my experience, those who struggle to know whether or not they are genuine believers do not often feel threatened by the first test in the way they feel menaced by the following two. The question, "Am I a godly person?" is a daunting question to answer if we are truly honest with ourselves. "Am I a loving person?" is also intimidating when I consider that the standard of love is the willing death of my Saviour. These two tests, flowing as they do out of the holy character of God, have often risen up to mock the profession of the man or woman who asks them.

How then should those who are struggling to know whether they are saved apply these tests to themselves? The answer is: In general, they should not apply them at all! (I will treat an exception to this general rule later.) The tests, speaking generally, are for those who are confident that they belong to Christ. They are for men and women who say that they have fellowship with Christ (1 John 1:6) and who affirm "I have come to know him" (1 John 2:4) and who claim to abide in him (1 John 2:6). They are for those who profess to walk in the light (1 John 2:9) and who may think of themselves as far enough along to teach others. These people, the ones with robust faith, are the ones to apply these tests to themselves.

Is there no help, then, for those with doubts and fears about their own salvation? Yes, much! Their help is found in taking their eyes off of themselves and directing them to Jesus Christ. In answer to the question, "What must I do to be saved?" Paul said, "Believe in the Lord Jesus, and you shall be saved" (Acts 16:31). He said this because he knew this truth: "For God so loved the world, that He gave His only begotten Son, that whoever believes in Him should not perish, but have eternal life" (John 3:16).

The problem of assurance is the problem of salvation. It is the agonizing question, "Do I belong to Christ or not?" The answer is the same in both cases: confident faith in Jesus Christ as Saviour and Lord. The tests are for those who say, "I am a Christian!" Those who had departed from John (and from Christ) were loud in their professions of faith. "Very well then," John said, "let us see. Let us test their faith. Let us test the faith of all of us who are sure that we belong to Christ. Here are the tests." And he followed with the tests of orthodoxy, godliness and love.

But poor trembling sinners need to turn their eyes solely to Jesus. The Puritan Thomas Willcox put it this way:

> If you have looked at words, duties and qualifications more than at the merits of Christ, it will cost you dearly. No wonder you go about complaining. Graces may be evidences; the merits of Christ alone (without the evidences) must be the foundation of your hope to stand on. Christ only can be the hope of glory (Colossians 1:27).
>
> When we come to God, we must bring nothing but Christ with us. Any ingredients, or any previous qualifications of our own, will poison and corrupt faith. He who builds upon duties, graces, etc., knows not the merits of Christ. Despairing sinner! Look at Christ now; look to him and be saved, all the ends of the earth (Isaiah 45:22). There is none else. He is the Saviour, and there is no other besides him (verse 21). Look anywhere else and you are undone. God will look at nothing but Christ and you must look at nothing else. This is the way to clear the fog of doubt and come into the sunshine of God's peace. In this way the holiness of God is not a threat to the soul.[1]

THE QUESTION OF ASSURANCE

What then of John's tests? Have they no use? Of course they have! For when the sinner or doubting saint has rested his or her case fully upon Christ, then comes the time to apply these tests. As a psychological state, or what I would call a state of mind, assurance, whether it comes from ourselves, or from God, or from Satan, is alike. John's tests come in precisely here; they are tests of our assurance. When the sinner no longer doubts about his interest in Christ, then is the time to test his assurance to see if it is soundly based.

We may summarize this in the following chart:

THE QUESTION OF ASSURANCE

STATE OF THE CHRISTIAN	EXPECTED ACTION
I have robust assurance that I belong to Jesus Christ	You must test the reality of your faith by the following texts: 1 John 2:4–6 [the test of godliness]; 1 John 2:9–11 [the test of love for Christian brothers].
I have doubts concerning whether I belong to Jesus Christ	You must act upon the following texts: Acts 16:31; John 3:16; Romans 4:5.

Everything, as you can see, depends on which row describes your situation. Are you without assurance? The second row applies to you. Do you have robust faith? The first row is where you must go.

"But," someone objects, "I can imagine myself bouncing back and forth between these two rows, first resting on Christ, and then having my faith dislodged repeatedly. What should I do?"

That case, of course, is easy to imagine, but is it likely to happen? I think not. Several things make it unlikely. To begin with, experience suggests that those who lack assurance and are serious about finding it in their godliness and love have not often drawn back and started over, as it were, by simply looking to Christ. If we are convinced that John's tests are the place to find our assurance we are likely to apply ourselves more persistently to their use as assurance falls. This is a losing strategy, increasing our discomfort. At this point we must return to first things. Faith in Christ is where healing lies.

Beyond that, an increase in concentration upon Christ is the best preparation, for both the production of godliness and its discovery in the life. Paul assures the Ephesians that the knowledge of the love of Christ is the grand basis of sanctification. He prays that they will learn the breadth and length and height and depth of the love of Christ "that you may be filled up to all the fullness of God" (Ephesians 3:19). God is filled with the most wonderful qualities. Some of them, those called communicable attributes by theologians, he gives in measure to his people. How will we be filled with these? Paul's answer is clear: We will receive them by concentrating on the love of Christ. And the more of these things that actually exist in us, the more easy they will be to discover.

Here are some other questions that may arise: First, how soon should one move from row two to row one? This is not a matter of time; it might be five minutes, it might be never. You must not take up the texts under row one until you can say that you have firm faith that you belong to Jesus Christ.

Second, suppose you have robust faith in Christ, but the texts in row one make you "uneasy." What should you do? The answer depends on what you mean by "uneasy." If you mean that you see shortcomings that you need to work on, go ahead and work on them. A Christian should be constantly striving against sin and self-satisfaction. But if by "uneasy" you mean that you have begun to doubt whether you are a Christian, you must forget the tests and take up the texts in row two.

Finally, are there any exceptions to the advice in this chapter to keep clear of the texts in row one unless you already have confident faith? There is one exception. Some people with little or no assurance are helped toward assurance by the tests in row one. If you are one of those people, by all means use them. But if that is not your case, you will only injure yourself by using row one. First, you must have firm faith in Christ.

Let me make one closing point. It is this: No amount of conformity to the will of God can ever bring you up to the full measure of God's holiness in this life. The Bible makes this very clear and, unfortunately, our daily experience confirms it. That raises a question: If I must always fall short of the standard set forth in the tests, of what use are they after all?

The answer to that question seems clear. The "tests" enable a man or woman to see the *fact* of God's working in his or her life, not the *extent* of God's work. All Christians are called "saints" in the New Testament. That means two things: First, it means they have been separated from the mass of mankind to belong to God. Second, it means that God, in that act of separation, has begun to make them like Christ in godliness and love. The important phrase in that last sentence is "has begun." No Christian has arrived at perfection. No two Christians are exactly the same distance along the road to pure holiness. The tests do not enable us to measure our progress with precision. But our assurance is not to rest on our superiority, real or imagined, over fellow believers. It is enough for us if we can see God at work. We need no more than that.

17

GOD'S FATHERHOOD
AND PRAYER

A moment's thought will show that God's nature—what he is like—plays a major role in prayer. There are two reasons for this. First, everything we do, everything we think, and our very existence depend on God. Were he a different God, we would be different people, or no people at all! Second, prayer is directed to God, not to others. When we pray, God is not a third party looking on, but the one who receives our prayers and deals with them as he sees fit. What he is like means everything.

Is he, for example, powerful? If not, our prayers are in vain. Theoretically no Christian can deny the power of God, but there is often just enough that is unique about our present circumstances to make us practically doubtful about his power to meet our specific need. That is why, in dealing with the Roman centurion whose servant was ill, Jesus treated belief in his power to heal as faith indeed (Matthew 8:5–10). When the centurion showed faith in Jesus' authority over sickness (or the forces necessary to eradicate

This essay first appeared in *Reformation & Revival Journal*, 7, No. 2 (Spring 1998), 79–88.

it), Jesus "marveled, and said…, 'I have not found such great faith with anyone in Israel'" (Matthew 8:10). Faith in God, like faith in Jesus, is in part faith in his ability, his power. You will see immediately that other attributes of God must also come into play in trusting him, such things as his goodwill toward you and his attention to your prayers (in theological terms, his omniscience). He must be a prayer-hearing God to be a prayer-answering God. One would be useless to prayer without the other. Yet the Bible shows that prayer, whether or not we grasp how it works, is anything but useless. Tennyson was on biblical ground when he wrote, "More things are wrought by prayer than this world dreams of." Is there a word that captures this relation of God to the prayers of his people? There is: the word *Father*. The word Father is too rich to confine to his relation to our prayers, of course. That is clear. Like all but the most technical terms, it means different things in different contexts. For example, it refers to the eternal relation between the Son as the second person of the Trinity and the Father as the first person. It has other uses as well.

The way the Lord Jesus treated his relation to his Father during his earthly ministry, however, offers us a model for our own thoughts of God's fatherhood, and nowhere is this more applicable than in our prayers. Our sonship to God is built on the analogy of his own sonship. He is "the firstborn among many brethren" (Romans 8:29). The firstborn in Israel was the chief heir, but his heirship did not exclude inheritance for other sons. Christ's people, then, are "children of God, and if children, heirs also, heirs of God and fellow heirs with Christ" (Romans 8:16–17). We are children by adoption into God's family and have received a spirit of adoption as sons [and daughters] by which we cry out, 'Abba! Father!'" (Romans 8:15; see also Galatians 4:5–7).

Among other things, this means that our prayers, especially in the way we address God, are to be modelled on Jesus' own prayers. Jesus used the name Father repeatedly in his own prayers (Matthew 26:39,42,44; John 17:1,5,11,21,24–25), and we are to do the same. The cry, "Father!" ("Abba" in his native Aramaic) must arise from our lips as from his. How do we know this? He told us so when he instructed his followers in prayer. "Pray, then, in this way: 'Our Father…' " (Matthew 6:9; 7:7–11; Luke 11:2; John 15:16; 16:23).

Left to itself, of course, this is a merely formal and relatively unimportant point. Men often use the right turn of phrase when it means little or nothing to them inwardly. Society oils the friction in human relations with formal language that may signify nothing. Think of the word *dear* in the phrase "Dear-John letter," a letter intended to say that John is not as *dear* as he once was! But very often formal language points beyond itself to heartfelt truth. Among those whose hearts have been changed by the Spirit of God, that is the case with Father.

A man, even an ungodly man, may certainly train himself to address God as Father. Theological talk earlier in the century spoke of the fatherhood of God and the brotherhood of man, thus encouraging this very thing. But to return to Paul in Romans 8, his point is more subtle. His view is that God has placed the impulse to call God "Father" in all who have been born again, as a cornerstone of our assurance that we are his. Suppose you are uncertain about your own salvation. The prayer "Father, I do not know if I am a Christian or not!" may show the reality of your relation to God. (Again, that will depend on whether you have taught yourself to say this, or whether "Father" arises as the natural impulse of your heart. No one should rest the weight of his or her assurance on using the right formal language.) How does the name "Father" bear on prayer?

In seed form, Jesus answers that question in his prelude to the Lord's Prayer: "And when you are praying, do not use meaningless repetition, as the Gentiles do, for they suppose that they will be heard for their many words. Therefore do not be like them; for your Father knows what you need, before you ask Him" (Matthew 6:7–8). Why did Jesus say this? Let us see if we can tease out the truths that cluster around the word *Father* here. (Note that fatherhood in the teaching of Jesus assumes the ideal that exists in God himself. Many earthly fathers have fallen so far short of this that *father* may have no pleasant associations for their children. But we must not let this put us off.)

To begin with, your Father listens to the cries of his children. Jesus makes this point in two ways. First, he tells you that you need not try to get God's attention. You may take "meaningless repetition" to stand for any technique to make the Father hear you: loud cries, pious looks, or "holy" postures. All are unnecessary! More than that, his "hearing" preceded your cry. He already knows your need.

This second detail, God's knowledge, deserves a closer look. Jesus' point is not academic; it is a word of encouragement. He does not mean to tell us that whether God helps us or not, he is well able to count up our needs. Not at all! We need no assurance that God is a good mathematician! The whole point is to say that the God who knows is the Father who provides. Take heart, Jesus says.

Let us look at the implications of this. First, it assures us of God's good will toward his people, his continuing love for us. Those who have faith in Christ are reconciled to God. That means that God and his people are friends. His friends and his children are one and the same. God acts toward his children as one ought to act toward friends. Let this idea soak into your mind! Because children receive discipline they may think that parents have, temporarily at least, become their enemies. But to say, "This man is my friend," leaves the whole idea of ill will far behind. The Lord loves his people more than we love our own children.

In telling you that "your Father knows what you need, before you ask him," Jesus assumes God's ability, that he is well able to supply your need. This is an advance on the faith of the centurion previously mentioned. Jesus had exhaustive knowledge of the Father (Matthew 11:27). He spoke not by faith but by sight. Three critical things meet in these words of the Lord: God's knowledge (he knows your need), God's good will (he loves his own) and God's power (he is well able to supply your need). You are to think of these things as you use the word "Father" in prayer. Because he is your Father, you will receive what you need.

Another thing comes into play here in connection with God as

Father—his wisdom. Think again of the words, "Your Father knows what you need, before you ask him." When children ask for things, they often ask amiss. That is true of us, as well. What you need and what you ask for, may be two different things. Often you do not remember that as you ask, but your Father does. This is a chief source of what we call "unanswered prayers," prayers to which the answer is "No." Why does our Father not give us all we ask for? Because he is too wise to do so.

To sum up the points we have already made, God's fatherhood includes his knowledge, goodwill, power and wisdom. Here is another point that bears on prayer. God's fatherhood includes his authority over us as we pray. When Christ prayed to his Father in Gethsemane he made this point repeatedly, "My Father, if it is possible, let this cup pass from Me; yet not as I will, but as Thou wilt" (Matthew 26:39; see also verses 42 and 44). He did not have to say, "as Thou wilt." It was already implied in the words, "if it is possible," but he made it explicit because he felt the need to openly recognize his Father's authority. "[N]ot My will, but Thine be done" (Luke 22:42).

There is an important lesson here for us. We may feel an intense emotional attachment to the idea that God is our Father because of the rich gifts we expect him to send us as his children. And there is nothing wrong with that. He has rich gifts; he does give them to us; they are a cause for rejoicing. Strong positive emotions, good feelings, both in anticipating what he will do for us and in enjoying what we have already received, are themselves gifts of God, not to be despised.

The word Father, however, must always carry with it the idea of his lordship over us. We may not use the sweet associations of the Father's love for us to aid us in disowning his rulership. He retains the right to thwart our desires for reasons that may utterly escape us. He may send us pain and circumstances that frustrate us. We must not act as spoiled children when this occurs. Instead we must seek to praise him for his sovereignty over us, while we rest in his wisdom and good will. Yes, we are his children, but we are children under discipline. "[I]f you are without discipline…then you are illegitimate children and not sons" (Hebrews 12:8).

> For they [our fathers] disciplined us for a short time as seemed best to them, but He disciplines us for our good, that we may share His holiness. All discipline for the moment seems not to be joyful, but sorrowful; yet to those trained by it, afterwards it yields the peaceful fruit of righteousness (Hebrews 12:10–11).

Once more, then, let me sum up: God's fatherhood, as it bears on prayer, includes his knowledge, goodwill, power, wisdom and authority.

There is another way to approach the subject of God as Father, however, besides listing his attributes. We may ask, "What person is it whom we address as 'Our Father'?" The obvious answer is the first person of the Trinity, the one we speak of when we distinguish Father, Son and Spirit. But is that answer correct?

At first this may seem a strange question indeed. To whom else could we be speaking? If you put yourself in the place of the disciples to whom Jesus gave instruction on prayer, you may readily see another possibility: God the Trinity. Distinctions that jump into our minds between the persons of the Trinity would have been lost on these men during Jesus' earthly ministry. When he said, "Our Father," they could have thought of no one except God without any further analysis. To them, his words meant, "Call God 'Our Father.' " Some theologians have thought that is what we do also. We call the entire Trinity "Our Father." That raises the far-reaching question, To what extent may further revelation and the tide of history alter the meaning of a text? At that time, trinitarian distinctions were unknown to them. Church councils that would adopt the word "Trinity" lay hundreds of years in the future. So what else could "Our Father" mean? Perhaps a small discussion of the process of interpreting Scripture will help here.

For the purpose of this study let us think of any text as containing three components: first, what the listener might reasonably have understood by it; second, what the inspired human speaker or writer meant by it; third, what God meant in giving it. Are all these things not the same?

The answer is yes and no. Acts of judgment aside (Isaiah 6:9–10; Matthew 13:10–15), we may assume that God intends for men to understand what he says (2 Corinthians 1:13). That means that "what the listener might reasonably have understood by it" falls within God's intention. Further, what the inspired speaker or writer meant also falls within God's intention. The intention of God, however, may be larger than the understanding of either the listener or the inspired writer or speaker. Nothing can change the intention of God, but later revelation and centuries of reflection on what God has said may broaden and deepen our understanding. What we now understand may be both true and fragmentary. Our present understanding may not exhaust the intention of God.

When Jesus used the words "Our Father," the disciples could not have understood a reference to anyone but God, without the distinctions of persons. Clearly, this was suitable to the intention of Jesus, or he would not have given this instruction, whether we think of him as speaking purely from his humanity, or whether we think of him as speaking as God. But God's revelation on this point was not yet complete. The materials in the New Testament demand differentiation of the persons, as later centuries defined them. The result is this: Intelligent Christians today, when they reflect on how they use "Our Father" in prayer, almost always refer to the first person of the Trinity. So which is it? Should we address the Father, as distinct from the Son and Spirit, when we say, "Our Father," or should we simply address God?

In the light of the rest of the New Testament we may answer by noting that prayer is usually addressed to the Father as distinct from the Son and the Spirit. That suggests we should follow suit, keeping the distinct persons in mind. (Compare this from the *Westminster Larger Catechism* where "God" appears to mean the first person of the Trinity: "Prayer is an offering up of our desires unto God, in the name of Christ, by the help of the Spirit.") Though prayer is directed to the Father primarily, we must not think that crying out to Christ or the Spirit is forbidden. Each of the persons has the knowledge, goodwill, power and wisdom to answer us and each exercises authority over us before, during and after prayer. (See the instances of prayer to the Lord Jesus in 1 Corinthians 16:22 and Revelation 22:20.)

We may fittingly close with these words from the *Heidelberg Catechism*, Question 120:

> Question: Why hath Christ commanded us to address God thus, "Our Father"?
> Answer: That immediately in the very beginning of our prayer, he might excite in us a childlike reverence for, and confidence in God, which are the foundations of our prayer; namely, that God is become our father in Christ, and will much less deny us what we ask of him in faith, than our parents refuse us earthly things.

To him be the glory!

18

WHAT SHOULD
WE PRAY FOR?

What should we pray for? I can imagine a certain frustration in reading that question. You might say something like this: "Surely a spiritual Christian does not need to ask that question. There are enough needs in the world to keep me busy for the rest of my life. There is food for prayer everywhere!" Of course, you would be quite right.

Nevertheless, I do not think you reacted that way to my question. Why not? I said that I could *imagine* such a frustration. The fact is, however, most Christians have more than once asked themselves, "What should I pray for?" without coming up with a satisfactory answer.

The early followers of Christ asked, "Lord, teach us to pray" (Luke 11:1). We may be tempted to write them off as babes in Christ, but mature Paul wrote to the Romans of our common weakness, "We do not know what we ought to pray for" (Romans 8:26). Why do we not know what to pray for? Let me suggest some reasons.

First, the number of choices seems to be infinite. For instance,

This essay first appeared in *Reformation & Revival Journal*, 1, No. 3 (Summer 1992), 55–64.

anything that it is right to want, it is right to pray for. Think of it! "You do not have, because you do not ask God," we read in James 4:2. Do you want something? As far as you can tell, is it a good thing? Then ask God! That is James' message. There you have a wide open door for literally millions of prayers, but that fact is likely to seem overwhelming when you think about it. How can you choose what to pray for, out of such a vast ocean of possibilities?

Here is a second thing that may hinder us in knowing what to pray for. Our theology may get in our way. Suppose we believe that God is sovereign and has decided what will happen in history. What difference, then, will our prayers make? Suppose we believe that man's free will is the decisive factor in day-to-day living. What can God do then? Are his hands not tied? From either perspective, we come upon important theological hindrances to prayer. Each of these views has its own ways of explaining why prayer is still meaningful, but they are not obvious to the casual observer. Just thinking about these things may keep us from choosing what we will pray for.

There is one kind of prayer, however, that bypasses these difficulties. I want to make it the subject of this article. I am speaking of *prayer that asks God to do precisely what he has already made up his mind to do.* The obvious advantage to this kind of prayer is that our prayers will always be answered, and the answer will always be yes! Has God made up his mind to send the Lord Jesus a second time to earth? Well, then, if you pray, "Father, send your Son back to earth," without specifying when or how, your prayer will be answered exactly as you prayed it. What more could you want? At this point you may think I am joking, or you may ask the question, "Does the Bible really teach us to pray prayers of this kind?" I have two answers to this question, and I think one of them will surprise you.

The first answer is yes it does. To stick with our illustration about the return of Christ, here is such a prayer: "Come, Lord Jesus" (Revelation 22:20).

The second answer is the surprising one. Most of the prayers in the New Testament are of this type; or, more accurately, most of the *petitions* of the New Testament are of this type. (Thanksgiving, which is also prayer, is very frequent.)

Take this prayer from 1 Thessalonians 5:23: "May God himself, the God of peace, sanctify you through and through. May your whole spirit, soul and body be kept blameless at the coming of our Lord Jesus Christ." Is this a prayer that might possibly be answered when Jesus comes? What are the chances that it will be heard? Paul tells us in the following verse, verse 24: "The One who calls you is faithful and He will do it." This prayer is a sample of the kinds of things Paul prays for all of his converts and for other Christians of whom he hears. It is clear that God does not work sanctification in every Christian in the same way or at the same pace, but it is equally clear that God will do this eventually in every believer.[1]

The clearest examples of what I am talking about, however, come from the prayers and teaching of the Lord Jesus. It is true, of course, that the Lord Jesus knew a great deal more than you and I do about the will of God. But the important thing is this: When he knew exactly what his Father was going to do, he prayed for it to happen anyway. Not only that, he taught his disciples to pray the same way.

Let us start with the Lord Jesus' own prayers. Listen to him praying in John 17: "Father, I want those you have given Me to be with Me where I am, and to see My glory, the glory You have given Me because You loved Me before the creation of the world" (John 17:24). His request is a simple one. He wants his followers to be with him in heaven. We might, perhaps, think that up to this point in his life, there was some doubt about that. Would they or would they not join him there? In fact there was no doubt about it at all. Earlier in the Gospel of John, Jesus had told his disciples:

> In My Father's house are many rooms; if it were not so, I would have told you. I am going there to prepare a place for you. And if I go and prepare a place for you, I will come back and take you to be with Me that you also may be where I am (John 14:2–3).

Nothing could be more definite than that, yet the Lord Jesus did not hesitate to pray that it might happen. In other words, he prayed for something that God had already made up his mind to do.

Before we try to find a rationale for this kind of prayer, let us see some further examples from the life of Jesus. Here are some words of Christ from John 14: "If you love Me, you will obey what I command. And I will ask the Father, and He will give you another Counselor to be with you forever—the Spirit of truth" (John 14:15–17a). We cannot doubt that the presence of the Spirit with Christ's followers was part of God's plan from the beginning. Yet here the Lord Jesus speaks of asking the Father to do what he has clearly already made up his mind to do.

This is the way the Lord Jesus instructed his own disciples to pray. After looking on the crowds that thronged him and feeling compassion for them, Jesus said to his followers: "The harvest is plentiful but the workers are few. Ask the Lord of the harvest, therefore, to send out workers into his harvest field" (Matthew 9:37b–38).

Here the Lord tells his disciples to pray for a central part of God's plan, the sending of workers to preach God's truth. God is the Lord of the harvest, according to Jesus. We must appeal to him to send forth labourers. Will he do so? Certainly he will. The very title, *Lord of the harvest*, shows that he has both power to raise up workers and power to control the extent of the harvest. We may not see immediately why we should ask, but the answer to that prayer is certain. The beginning of its fulfillment is found in the following chapter where the Lord Jesus sends out the Twelve to preach and to heal.

I have not yet come, however, to the clearest example of praying that God will do what he has already decided to do. That example is the Lord's Prayer as given to us in Matthew 6:9–13:

> "Our Father in heaven, hallowed be Your name, Your kingdom come, Your will be done on earth as it is in heaven. Give us today our daily bread. Forgive us our debts, as we also have

forgiven our debtors. And lead us not into temptation, but deliver us from the evil one."

We have all known this prayer for many years, and we may also know a good deal about its contents. So far, so good. But have you ever looked at the Lord's Prayer from this perspective: What are the chances of these petitions being answered? As far as I can see, the answer is this: *God will do* all of these things. Not one of them shall fail.

How about the first request, "Hallowed be Thy name?" Is that going to happen? Certainly it will. God will see to it that he is glorified in all the universe, through both men and angels as well as through the created world. God has made up his mind that it will happen, and nothing on earth will stop it from happening.

Let us take the next request, "Your kingdom come." Will it come? It surely will! That will be true even though Christians are not fully agreed on what that prayer means. They do agree on this: Whatever it means, God will surely do it! God's kingdom will come.

The third petition is this: "Your will be done on earth as it is in heaven." Again there is not full agreement on the meaning of this request. Is it another way of asking that God's kingdom would come? Is it a prayer for a future millennium? These are hard questions, but one thing is sure: God's will will be done on earth sooner or later, whether in a millennial kingdom or in the new heavens and the new earth. All sides agree that this prayer will be answered even though we are still praying it after two thousand years.

Let us look at the fourth request, "Give us today our daily bread." Will the Lord do that? Yes, he will. It is true that he may see that we need the discipline of going hungry, and then he may withhold our bread. But many exegetes have seen *bread* here as representative of our daily needs generally. The Lord Jesus taught us that God is a Father to his spiritual children. What does a father do? He provides his children's needs. In this same context, in fact, Jesus taught us that we need not "keep on babbling like pagans...for your Father knows what you need before you ask Him" (Matthew 6:7–8). It is clear that Jesus was not just supplying academic information when he said that. The point was plain: Your Father is going to look after you; that is what a father does!

The fifth request asks for the forgiveness of our sins. Will God forgive our sins? The answer lies at the heart of the gospel: Yes, he will. Again, Christians have understood this forgiveness in various ways, but most have seen that without the perpetual forgiveness of our sins there would be no Christians. "We all stumble in many ways" (James 3:2a). If our sins are to be unforgiven, we will be lost forever! [2]

The final request goes like this: "And lead us not into temptation, but deliver us from the evil one."[3] Will the Lord deliver us from Satan? If we are saved, he has already done so to some degree. As Paul told the Colossians, God "has rescued us from the dominion of darkness [the devil's kingdom] and brought us into the kingdom of the Son he loves" (Colossians 1:13). More than that, he will perfect that work, so that all the power of Satan over us will be broken forever. That was the very purpose for which the Lord Jesus came. John wrote in his first letter, "The reason the Son of God appeared was to destroy the devil's work" (1 John 3:8b). We need not doubt that he will do it!

The conclusion is clear: An important part of prayer is praying that God will do what he has already made up his mind to do. A corollary blessing is this: If we pray this way, the answer will be yes one hundred percent of the time!

Let me close by taking up the question: "Why would anyone pray for the things that God is going to do, whether we pray or not? What is the point of that?"

First, you may have noticed that I have subtly changed the question here. We were not discussing what God would do *whether we pray or not*. We were discussing what God will certainly do. How do those two ideas differ? They differ in this way: One of them assumes that God had not already taken our prayers into consideration when he formed his plans. There is no reason to assume that. While he was planning everything else he was going to do and allow, he no doubt included our prayers. In that way our prayers can be seen as really affecting something in the total outworking of God's purposes. He did not plan everything else and leave to chance whether or not we would pray. He planned to move us to pray as well. Millions upon millions of Christians have prayed the prayers we have looked at. They have asked him to send forth labourers; they have repeated the Lord's Prayer; they have focused on "Your will be done."

But there is more, much more. Many people have adopted the slogan "Prayer changes things!" They are right in one sense—a subsidiary sense—and wrong in another sense—a primary and fundamental sense.

Does prayer change things? Indeed it does! But it does not change the plans of God. When he made his plans he included among them the prayers of his people. In answer to prayer he changes events and circumstances from what they were, but he planned to do that all along! Any other kind of change would be suicidal to the human race. Why? Because God's plans, the things he chose to do or to allow, arose from infinite wisdom. Does any Christian seriously want to change that? Surely not! The world would love to change God's plans. That much is clear. But any man, woman, or child who has prayed, "Your will be done," does not want God to change anything that he has planned to do or allow. We may ask with Paul, "Who has been his counsellor?" (Romans 11:34). Paul did not ask this in despair, as though God would need advice. No, Paul asked it in leading up to the doxology in verse 36, "To Him be glory forever!"

What is the role of the prayer that asks God to do what he has already made up his mind to do? Why would anyone pray such a prayer?

Let me answer with an illustration. The illustration is trivial in itself, but it does illustrate the point. Suppose you are at a football game and your team has been pushed back near their own goal line. What will happen next? One thing that is likely to happen is this: Cheerleaders and others may begin chanting, "Hold that line! Hold that line!" Now let me ask you a question about that chant. Is it a piece of advice to the team to change their plans? Hardly! But if it is not that, what is it? Those who are cheering are not giving the team advice; they are encouraging the team to do what the team has already planned to do! They are encouraging the team by saying, in effect, "Go for it! Do your thing! Carry out your plan! Put it into action!"

That is what the Christian is to do in prayer. A Christian is a *God-admirer*. More than anything else, he wants God to carry out his plans and to do his will. No, that is not all that prayer is about. There is a place for asking God to do things when we have no idea what his will is. We may pray for healing, for example, if it is his will. I do not want to discourage that, any more than I would want to discourage praise and thanksgiving to God in prayer. All these things go together to make up Christian prayer.

But in a day of man-centeredness, when man is the measure of all things in the eyes of many, we who are Christians must be careful. Our business is not to follow the world in preoccupation with ourselves. Neither is it our business to give God advice. The great want of every age is God-centered men and women. We need them. You and I need to be such people. How will God-centered men and women pray? They will pray as those who admire the infinite wisdom of God; they will ask God to do his own will first of all. In doing that, they will follow the example of Scripture. What if you and I prove to be such people? What then? Then we will cheer God on by asking him to do precisely what he has already made up his mind to do. And we will do it with enthusiasm, as admirers of God.

19

THINKING CRITICALLY
ABOUT REVIVAL

A group of us were sitting around a table at our monthly pastors fellowship in Dayton, Ohio, agilely flitting from subject to subject when someone mentioned revival. The ensuing discussion went something like this: "What about the revival in China?" The question was directed to a missionary who had visited the People's Republic no less than ten times in recent years to evangelize college students in one of the major cities.

"You cannot believe what you hear coming out of China," was the reply. "I have seen nothing to confirm the stories of miracles that you may have heard of here in the States." He went on to cite an exciting story of superhuman endurance under trial by a Chinese believer. It was a good story, but it was false. Someone else chimed in. "But we have heard that there are fifty million Christians in China now. Is that true?"

"Yes," replied our friend, "that is true if you count all those who profess any kind of Christianity. Fifty million would be a

This essay first appeared in *Reformation & Revival Journal*, 4, No. 3 (Summer 1995), 59–64.

fair estimate."

I remember this exchange because it well illustrates the difficulty we have in understanding one another. When the missionary heard the word "revival," he assumed the question was about the exciting and the miraculous. But others heard a question about the vast numbers of men and women who have turned to Christ in China in the past twenty-plus years. It took a few minutes to unravel the confusion and to get us all thinking along the same lines.

Questions about the meaning of revival are not uncommon. Maybe you have heard a conversation that went something like this: "Revival occurs when God brings a large number of people to himself, when, in other words, men and women are being born again." "Not so fast! You cannot revive what has never been alive. Revival is a work among the people of God. Dead sinners do not come into it at the earliest stage." Clearly there is a difference here, but who is right and who is wrong?

I suspect that the answer lies in associating our present use of the term with a text like, "O Lord, revive Thy work in the midst of the years" (Habakkuk 3:2). Whenever God is unusually and powerfully at work in his world, there we rightly speak of revival. If we want to think critically about revival, then, we will concentrate on times and places where God is manifestly at work. I suppose there will not be much controversy about this.

But the first thing we have to think critically about shows that my own definition of revival, though accurate as far as it goes, begs an important question, "When is God manifestly at work?" Let me show you what I mean.

Let us compare the world as it exists today with the world at the end of the eighteenth century. At that time the knowledge of Christ was largely confined to the West. But then came the beginning of what has been called "the Modern Missionary Movement." Since that time the gospel has been carried to every part of the globe, and millions upon millions of men and women have been saved. If this is not an evidence of God reviving his work we would be hard pressed to identify such evidence anywhere in history.

It appears, then, that all of us are living within a time of revival, though we may have never thought of it in those terms. And this fact suggests an important ingredient in thinking critically about revival: Regardless of the claims that we may hear, identifying a revival demands time for reflection. A present claim that revival is happening may be true or it may be false. Only time will tell.

That does not mean, of course, that we must stand aloof from an apparent unusual work of God, but it does lead to an important question we must ask about what appears to be revival: Are prayer and the preaching of Jesus Christ prominent parts of what is happening? We understand, I think, that conversions do not come, men and women are not born again, except in connection with preaching and teaching about the Lord Jesus. "How shall they believe in him whom they have not heard? And how shall they hear without a preacher?" (Romans 10:14). We may add that progress in the Christian life, whether dramatic or more pedestrian, arises from the same source. We seek to "grow in the grace and in the knowledge of our Lord and Saviour Jesus Christ" (2 Peter 3:18). We expect to find growth in grace and in knowledge proceeding hand-in-hand. Men and women who are labouring to see revival may be doing what they would normally be doing: praying and spreading the knowledge of God in Christ. True, they may be doing it with extraordinary intensity, but these are the two instruments to which God has promised blessing.

Let me add a final point that will help us think both critically and sympathetically about revival: It is no proof that a revival does not exist just because it is accompanied by significant abuses. Men's carnality often gets mixed in with undoubted works of God.

Let us take an example from that movement of God called the First Great Awakening. The story of abuses fostered by James Davenport has often been told, but let us consider another figure, a far more central figure than Davenport, the preacher Gilbert Tennent, a man whose memory is honoured by all those who are friends of revival. Tennent was an earnest servant of Christ, greatly used of God, but in the matter we are about to examine he was a man "who acted more from feeling than from principle." And his feelings reached fever pitch when he thought he saw opposition or indifference to the revival in his brother ministers. Where less confident men would have hesitated, he knew exactly what he would do. He published what has come to be known as his "Nottingham Sermon" on unconverted ministers, "which is one of the most terrible pieces of denunciation in the English language."

Two things made this sermon odious to many of his fellow ministers. First, Tennent urged the lawfulness of leaving the ministry of any pastor who was godly but had inferior gifts. There might have been some logic to this plea if he had used the inferiority of their gifts to show that they were not called to the ministry. But that was not his point, as we may see from the illustration he uses of many leaving John the Baptist to follow Christ.

Second, Tennent argued from his first point in these words: "If it be lawful to withdraw from the ministry of a pious man...how much more from the ministry of a natural man? Surely it is both lawful and expedient..."

We are not surprised to hear a gospel minister urge us to turn from the ministry of hypocrites. But what made his exhortation so prejudicial to the cause of revival was his application of this rule to a large number of ministers who were sound in doctrine and gave every appearance of being godly men except for their lack of enthusiasm for the awakening. In fact, many of them might have been brought around in time, but treating them as enemies of God strengthened their resolve to have nothing to do with Tennent and those who thought like him.

The result of Tennent's intemperate zeal leaped across the bounds of individual lives to split the Presbyterian denomination into two churches, a wound that was not healed for seventeen years (1741–1758). Yet the revival was real, and Tennent was a man greatly used of God.

Years later Tennent himself helped to heal the wound by recognizing the folly his otherwise-commendable zeal had led him into. In his *Irenicum Ecclesiasticum* he wrote that his earlier denunciation of his brother ministers was:

> an evil pregnant with pride, malice, and mischief, though
> perhaps not perceived or intended; an evil, which under a
> cloak of misguided zeal for God...[and] under the pretext of
> kindness and piety, cruelly rends our neighbor's character,
> saps the foundation of the church's peace, and turns its union,
> order, and harmony, into the wildest confusion of
> ungoverned anarchy, schism, prejudice, and hate.

Thus ended a sad chapter in the history of genuine revival.

Let me review, in reverse order, the three tests of revival I have
laid out:

1) The presence of abuse does not prove that a revival is not of God.
I have cited a denunciatory attitude toward fellow believers as
one such abuse. There have been many others. In fact, there are
many others in what often passes for revival in our own day.
These things in themselves do not prove the absence of the
Spirit of God. They do, however, alert us in two ways: first, to
have nothing to do with the excesses as far as we can determine
what they are, and second, to apply the next test.

2) We should expect true revival to engage men in both prayer and
supreme emphasis on Jesus Christ. The absence of these things
is fatal to any claim of revival. We hear pleas today to believe that
roarings and infectious laughter signal the presence of revival.
But are they the results of careful exposition of the Lord Jesus as
our Prophet, Priest and King? When the apparent author or
chief promoter of the current craze for laughter tells jokes in
public meetings to prompt it, it is not hard to know what to
think. And when he defends it on the ABC television network by
pleading that since people laugh longer at his jokes than the jokes
themselves warrant, it shows that the Holy Spirit is the source of
the laughter, we may be excused for being skeptical.

3) We often need the perspective of years to make a final judgment. At the end of the day the passage of time will settle the issue in two ways. First, it will help us to examine the lasting influence of the revival. Are the participants more godly today than they were then? If they were among the abusers of revival, have they owned their abuses as both James Davenport and Gilbert Tennent did? Questions like these cannot be answered immediately.

Second, the passage of time will bring us to the judgment of the infallible Judge. There we will learn the verdict of the One with infinite wisdom. His will be the final court of appeal. In the meantime we will continue to suspect with Austin Phelps that

> if the secret connections of revivals with the destiny of nations could be disclosed, they would appear to be more critical evolutions of history than the Gothic invasions. A volume has been compiled, narrating the decisive battles of the world. But more significant than this, and probing deeper the Divine government of the world, would be the history of revivals.

SECTION IV

Biography

20

SAMUEL PEARCE
1766–1799

Writing perhaps fifty years after the death of Samuel Pearce, the English Congregational preacher William Jay (1769–1853) set down these striking words:

> It may seem to be saying much, but I speak the words of truth and soberness,—when I have endeavoured to form an image of our Lord as a preacher, Pearce has oftener presented himself to my mind than any other I have been acquainted with… I cannot accurately convey the appearance and impression he made, yet I can see the one, and feel the other, even at this great distance of time.[1]

Two things make this statement remarkable. First, as a preacher of eminent usefulness, Jay was no mean judge of preaching talents. Of Jay's own preaching Charles Spurgeon (1834–1892) once wrote, "Matthew Henry is Jay writing, Jay is Matthew Henry

This essay first appeared in Michael A.G. Haykin, ed., *The British Particular Baptists, 1638–1910* (Springfield, Missouri: Particular Baptist Press, 2000), II, 182–199.

preaching. What more could I say in commendation of the preacher or the author?"[2] We may hear his judgment on Pearce, then, with more than passing interest. Equally remarkable, however, is the fact that these words were spoken of a man largely forgotten today, even among Baptists. Who is this man who came to be called "the seraphic Pearce," and what may we learn from him today?

EARLY YEARS

Samuel Pearce was born in the south of England at the port city of Plymouth on July 20, 1766. While he was yet an infant his mother died, and he went to live with his grandparents until he was eight or nine years old, returning to his father at that age to begin to learn his father's trade of silversmith. Both his parents and grandparents were devout Christians, and he had the benefit of godly instruction in each home.

His later memories of his own moral inclinations as a boy were not happy ones, but with his conversion at age sixteen he felt himself transformed inwardly. Of this experience he said,

> I believe few conversions were more joyful. The change produced in my views, feelings, and conduct was so evident to myself, that I could no more doubt of its being from God than of my existence. I had the witness in myself, and was filled with peace and joy unspeakable.[3]

This expression of powerful emotion was not untypical of the inward life of Pearce, whose ardent feelings were now settled decisively on the Lord Jesus. Nevertheless he was capable of the opposite extreme of fear and distress at his own failures, though he clearly rested in Christ as the characteristic of his brief remaining seventeen years of life.

Although what appear to be wonderfully joyful conversion experiences often prove illusory, in Pearce's case it was not so. Within four years the Plymouth Baptist church where he had been converted and of which he was a member recognized in him gifts and graces needed for public ministry and called him as a probationer. Shortly after, he went to the Bristol Baptist Academy where he studied from 1786 to 1789.[4] As at Plymouth, so also at Bristol—his gifts were recognized, and at the end of his studies came an opportunity for regular ministry.

CANNON STREET BAPTIST CHURCH, BIRMINGHAM

Toward the end of 1789, he came to the Baptist church in Cannon Street, Birmingham, to whom he was recommended by Robert Hall, Jr., who at that time was one of his tutors. After preaching to them for a while, he was chosen to be their pastor. Caleb Evans, the principal of the Baptist Academy gave the charge, and Robert Hall, Sr., of Arnesby, delivered an address to the church on the occasion.[5]

In February, 1791, Samuel Pearce married Sarah Hopkins of Alcester, twenty miles or so south of Birmingham. In her he found a companion who brought him joy through the rest of his life. The evidence is written plainly in his letters to home when he was travelling. For example, he wrote her from Plymouth, September 2, 1794:

> To-morrow morning I set off for Launceston. I write tonight, lest my stay in Cornwall might make my delay appear tedious to the dear and deserving object of my most undissembled love. O my Sarah, had I as much proof that I love *Jesus Christ* as I have of my love to *you*, I should prize it more than rubies! As often as you can find an hour for correspondence, think of your more than ever affectionate—S.P.[6]

Sarah's devotion to Samuel appears at the end of his race when she carefully recorded many of the words of his last four or five weeks.[7]

Pearce's ministry at Cannon Street prospered from the beginning. In the first two-and-a-half years he saw perhaps thirty or more converts to Christ,[8] but their numbers grew as the years went on. Michael Haykin has written:

His ministry at Cannon Street occupied ten all-too-brief years, yet they were ones of great fruitfulness. No less than 335 individuals were baptized during his ministry and received into the membership of Cannon Street. This figure does not include those converted under his preaching who, for one reason or another, did not join themselves to the Birmingham cause. A Sunday School was started in 1795 and soon grew to the point that some 1200 scholars were enrolled in it.[9]

THE BAPTIST MISSIONARY SOCIETY

Apart from his pastoral ministry, the high point in Pearce's life was his engagement in the founding and promotion of the Particular Baptist Society for Propagating the Gospel among the Heathen (later known simply as the Baptist Missionary Society). We now know the formation of this society to be the major catalyst of what has been called "the modern missionary movement." No inkling of its future fame could have been guessed in its humble beginnings, but Pearce threw himself into the project with the same godly zeal he would have shown had he been a seer.

The society's beginnings were humble enough and, from a human point of view, not at all promising. The formative meeting on October 2, 1792, was held in the small parlour of the house of a Mary Wallis, in Kettering, a room where three or four men might have met comfortably though there were fourteen wedged into it that day. Twelve of these men were pastors and most were, in S. Pearce Carey's words, "pastors of obscure little village causes" and men "of no fame and of scantiest salary."[10] Moreover, Andrew Fuller, who took charge of the meeting, had in successive weeks just prior to the meeting seen his wife lose her mind, give birth to an infant daughter, and die, to be followed in death by the infant about four weeks later.[11] When the men were asked to pledge funds for the undertaking, they could muster among themselves only a trifle over £13. Yet, Pearce and the others took heart at these small beginnings in the knowledge that God can work by many or by few, with much or with little.

Pearce's first act on returning to his congregation was to lay the project before them with so much enthusiasm that the Cannon Street church immediately subscribed an additional £70 for the society. In addition, under his leadership, a number of the leading members constituted themselves an assistant society to help forward the work.

Pearce did more for the Missionary Society than address his own congregation. Once there were missionaries to go to India he took it upon himself to raise funds elsewhere by travelling on the mission's behalf, including two trips to London, and by writing letters. Once more we see his ardent feelings displayed in this good work. In writing to his friend William Steadman, he rejoices in their common interest in the spread of the gospel. The two subjects, feelings and funds, meet here:

> [W]e feel alike respecting the poor heathens. Oh how Christianity expands the mind! What tenderness for our poor fellow sinners! What sympathy for their moral misery! What desires to do them everlasting good doth it provoke! ...Oh how I love that man whose soul is deeply affected with the importance of the precious gospel to idolatrous heathens! ...We shall be glad of all your assistance in a pecuniary way, as the expense will be heavy.[12]

In October 1794, Pearce took a further step; he told some of his fellow pastors of his desire to join William Carey and his fellow missionary, John Thomas (1757–1801), in India. In considering this proposal, he naturally struggled with the question of his duties, not only to India, but also to his local congregation and to his beloved Sarah in the event she would not follow him. As recently as 1959 a document containing some of these struggles was published for the first time by the English historian, Ernest A. Payne. In it Pearce reminds himself that he must be at the command of the Christ who has said that a man must be willing to forsake his wife if he would be Christ's disciple, and he steels himself for the possibility. Nevertheless he is happily able to add:

> But such a trial I have not in prospect. My wife says she will accompany me if I go, though reluctantly, and at times she has owned she herself feels as though she could be willing to take a part in the work...[13]

Having carefully weighed the possibilities, he could not be easily put off:

> [N]othing would satisfy him short of his making a formal offer of his services to the committee: nor could he be happy for them to decide upon it without their appointing a day of solemn prayer for the purpose, and, when assembled, hearing an account of the principal exercises of his mind upon the subject, with the reasons which induced him to make the proposal, as well as the reasons alleged by his connexions [sic] against.[14]

But it was no use. His friends agreed to his terms, but when the day had passed they had denied his request. "[A]s his ministry had been almost one continual revival of religion, and his counsel seemed necessary in the successful management of the society, he was dissuaded from going."[15]

In connection with this disappointment, we may quote some further words of Fuller: "There appears throughout the general tenor of his life a singular submissiveness to the will of God; and, what is worthy of notice, *this disposition was generally most conspicuous when his own will was most counteracted.*"[16] Of how many believers could this be said?

LATER MINISTRY

In the summer of 1796, Pearce was privileged to preach the gospel for more than four weeks during June and July in Dublin, Ireland, at the invitation of the General Evangelical Society of that city.

There, at the outset of his meetings, he met with another disappointment. Not only was attendance at his meetings somewhat sparse, but even the Evangelicals of the city, including his fellow Baptists, seemed more preoccupied with the fashions of the hour than with following Christ. But, before his month was done, the tide had turned. The change came with plain speaking on his part. In writing to Sarah (June 30, 1796) he said that he told his hearers "that if they made custom and fashion their plea, they were awfully deluding their souls; for it had always been the fashion to insult God, to dissipate time, and to pursue the broad road to hell: but it would not lessen their torments there that the way to damnation was the fashion." Then he added:

> I feared my faithfulness would have given them offence: but I am persuaded, it was the way to please the Lord; and those who I expected would be enemies are not only at peace with me, but even renounce their sensual indulgences to attend my ministry. I do assuredly believe that God hath sent me hither for good.[17]

Some indication of his usefulness in Ireland is also found in an invitation he shortly received to make his permanent home there, accompanied by the most generous offer of support. When he refused that offer, he was asked to consider six months a year and, later, at least three months. But he declined in each case, showing that his willingness to go to India was no evidence that he had lost his love for his beloved praying congregation in Cannon Street.

The final three years of Pearce's life were consistent with his burning passions to love God supremely and to wear himself out in the cause of Christ in the local church and in world missions. And "burn himself out" is what he did! A later assessment tells the tale. "Prodigal of his strength and health," write David Bogue and James Bennett, "he not only preached very frequently, but took many journeys, which exposed him to colds; and, unable to arrest for a moment his rapid course, he preached while his lungs were dangerously affected, so that, at length, he sunk under a consumption."[18]

Pearce woke up too late to what he was doing to himself. In his own words to a friend in March 1799, "I was rapidly destroying the vital principle."[19] And so, on December 2, 1798, four months before he wrote that saddest of lines, he preached his final sermon. Indeed, by this time he barely had breath for conversation. Hardly ever has a voice been more missed among a man's contemporaries. It pleased the Lord to allow him to live until October 10, 1799 and the spirit with which he met death gave to Andrew Fuller the opening lines of the *Memoir* from which we have often quoted:

> It was observed by this excellent man, during his affliction, that he never till then gained any personal instruction from our Lord's telling Peter by *what death* he should glorify God. To die by a consumption [i.e., pulmonary tuberculosis] had used to be an object of dread to him; but, "O my dear Lord," said he, "if by *this death* I can most *glorify thee*, I prefer it to all others."[20]

PEARCE'S DOCTRINE

When we come to assess the teaching of this much-used man of God, we meet at once the central fact: His doctrine was orthodox Christianity of the variety known as "experimental Calvinism." It is worth pausing for a moment over those two descriptive words, *experimental Calvinism*.

As late as the time of his birth in 1766, much of English Calvinism, including not a few Baptists, was languishing under the influence of views inimical to calling sinners indiscriminately to Christ, views that are sometimes called "High Calvinism."[21] Already the Presbyterians had had their "Marrow Controversy" (c.1717–1722) over similar issues.[22] Since all Calvinists taught the inability of the sinner to come to God, some concluded that the sinner had no responsibility to either repent or believe. They spoke against what came to be called "duty faith" and "duty repentance." This denial of "duty" came to be adopted by many Baptists in the early part of the eighteenth century.

It produced, in turn, a discussion over which of these positions was really *the* Calvinistic position. Samuel Pearce was firmly on the side of those who plainly commanded all men to repent and believe. In fact, his personal history was entwined with this problem by his association with the mission society.

Today, we take mission societies for granted, but the existence of the Particular Baptist Society was a tribute to the success of a group of Baptists in overcoming two obstacles that precluded the idea of such a society for many years.

First Andrew Fuller had overcome his own doubts about the propriety of preaching to all sinners and had published his findings in a landmark volume whose title tells its theme, *The Gospel Worthy of All Acceptation*. His friends, many of whom later joined in the formation of the mission society, were convinced that all are commanded by God to respond to the gospel.

Second Fuller and the others, including Pearce, had to be convinced of the practicability of preaching beyond their local stations. Here Carey, having imbibed the principles of Fuller and having compared them with the commission of Matthew 28:18–20, made a major contribution with a treatise of his own. Again the title tells the story, *An Enquiry into the Obligation of Christians, to Use Means for the Conversion of the Heathens*. Carey answered his own "Enquiry" with a resounding "Yes!" If we are commanded to go into all the world with the gospel and if the promise of Christ's presence for this purpose lasts through till the end of the age, then the church's duty in every generation is clear. The command itself assumes its own practicability.

Pearce entered wholeheartedly into the spirit of Carey's message as we have seen, even to the point of offering himself as a missionary. This, in his view, was one facet of real orthodoxy and Calvinism.

In addition, Pearce was an *experimental* Calvinist, one who sought to feel the impact of his theology by meditating upon the blessed truths of God given to all who have been effectually called to Christ. In this and many other things he and his circle had been greatly influenced by the writings of the American theologian,

Jonathan Edwards.[23] Marrying the affections and the intellect, they would have affirmed with Edwards,

> There is not only a rational belief that God is holy, and that holiness is a good thing, but there is a sense of the loveliness of holiness. There is not only a speculatively judging that God is gracious, but a sense of how amiable God is upon that account, or a sense of the beauty of this divine attribute.[24]

This marriage of feeling with truth is seen on every page of the adult life of Pearce. A few samples follow. In a letter to his friend, Mr. Summers, he says,

> I have of late had my mind very pleasantly, and I hope profitably, exercised on this subject, more than ever, and find increasing pleasure from a well-grounded faith in the *Divinity* of my incarnate Advocate. I see the glory of his office, arising from the infinite extent of his knowledge, power, and love, as well as from the efficacy of his atoning sacrifice. ...I rejoice in that he who pleads for us knows our wants individually, as well as the necessities of the whole church collectively. Through his intercession alone I expect my sins to be pardoned, my services accepted, and my soul preserved, guided, and comforted.... Oh how sweet it is, my dear friend, to exercise a lively faith in a living Saviour! May you and I do this daily.[25]

Writing to the same friend on September 30, 1791, he tells of preparing to preach on redemption:

> I have for my evening discourse the best subject in all the Bible. Eph. i.7—Redemption! how welcome to the captive! Forgiveness! how delightful to the guilty! ...[T]he atonement for sinners by the Son of God [is] a truth consonant with the yearnings and hopes of the earliest ages...adapted to blend the Divine perfections in the sinner's salvation, and above all

calculated to beget the most established peace, to inspire with the liveliest hope, and to engage the heart and life in habitual devotedness. Such a doctrine I cannot but venerate; and to the Author of such a Redemption my whole soul labours to exhaust itself in praise. *I cannot on this subject control my passions by the laws of logic.* God forbid that I should glory save in the Cross of Christ Jesus my Lord.[26]

And here we find him thinking on the sovereignty of God in his final afflictions and mixing in a heavy dose of joy in the hand that afflicts him:

My Master has no need of me just now, or he would not silence me; but I am in good hands; and in the midst of my imprisonment can shout with joy unspeakable, "Hallelujah; for the Lord reigneth." I am perfectly satisfied with His blessed will; *nor would I have it otherwise, were an alteration in my power...*[N]ow I know that God can render submission as happy as exertion, and call forth the passive graces to as good purpose as the most active ones. O sweet affliction! I would not have been without this trial for the Indies; it has taught me more of my Bible and my God than seven years' study could have done.[27]

And in the same final affliction he writes to Fuller

Thanks be to God who giveth my heart the victory. In the thought of leaving I feel a momentary gloom; but in the thought of going a heavenly triumph. Let every Christian sing the loudest, as he draws nearest to the Presence of his Lord.[28]

THE SIGNIFICANCE OF HIS LIFE

When we come to weigh the significance and influence of Pearce we find that both his character and spirit made a lasting impression on his generation. Scarcely had his single pastorate and brief life closed than John Ryland of Bristol named him "the seraphic." Men felt at once the fitness of the name, which ranked him with those "burning ones," and ever since, this crown has rested on his brow. "He is another Brainerd," exclaimed Andrew Fuller upon hearing of his death, and his *Memoirs* of his friend soon proved it. Of those *Memoirs*, Stephen Albert Swaine bears witness: "The whole range of Christian biography presents us with no such portraiture of endearing saintliness, except perhaps Dr. Bonar's Life of the sainted Robert Murray McCheyne."[29] And T.C. Skeats, the historian of the Free Churches declares: "No church ever possessed a man of holier character than Samuel Pearce. He was to the Baptists what [John] Fletcher was to the Methodists. His friends compared him to the disciple 'whom Jesus loved.' Wherever he went, the beauty of holiness accompanied him."[30]

We may start with *the breadth of his sympathies*. In Fuller's words, "He bore good will to all mankind."[31] We have seen this in his desire to go to India as a missionary, but it is also evident in some of the springs of that desire. A Methodist clergyman, Thomas Coke (1747–1814) played a role. Pearce "always dated his final and never-abating enthusiasm [for foreign missions] from the hearing, not long after his settlement in Birmingham, in the Cherry St. Methodist Church, a missionary sermon by the illustrious Dr. Coke...the "Foreign Minister of Methodism."[32]

Another source of inspiration was Lutheran. On receiving a print of Christian Frederick Schwartz (1726–1798), a missionary to southern India, he profusely thanked the friend who gave it, writing, "It represented a man whom I have long been in the habit of loving and revering."[33] It was this sanctified love to mankind that led him to throw himself heart and soul into the mission society.

Again the young were as dear to him as the old. In Fuller's words, "He was affectionate to all. but especially towards the *rising generation*,...While at Plymouth he wrote thus to one of his friends, 'Oh how should I rejoice, were there a speedy prospect of my returning to my great and *little* congregations'."[34]

He loved the poor. "His ministry was highly acceptable to persons of education; but he appears to have been most in his element when preaching to the poor," wrote Fuller. And he added, "[H]e both laboured and suffered to relieve their temporal wants; living himself in a style of frugality and self-denial, that he might have whereof to give to them that needed."[35]

Another facet of his character that impressed his contemporaries was *his joy*, constitutional to be sure, but greatly animated by thoughts of Christ and Christian truth. "Cheerfulness was as natural to him as breathing," Fuller commented, "and this spirit, sanctified by the grace of God, gave tincture to all his thoughts, conversation, and preaching. ...Religion in him was habitual seriousness, mingled with sacred pleasure, frequently rising into sublime delight, and occasionally overflowing with transporting joy."[36]

With all the adulation and praise that came his way, Pearce was remembered for *his modesty*. We see it not only in his declining the rich offer to settle in Ireland but also his never mentioning it, so that it became known among his circle of friends only after his death. In a memorial sermon preached on October 27, 1799, Andrew Fuller told his own people:

> For my own part, I never knew a man in whom were more united the contemplative and the active; the spiritual and the rational; talents which attracted almost universal praise, yet the most unaffected modesty...and gentleness that would not break a bruised reed...[37]

After Pearce's death, his friends shared with one another his correspondence and the deep impressions he had made on them individually. The effect was one that Pearce himself would have neither desired nor understood, a sense of unworthiness when compared with him. On reading Fuller's memoir, William Steadman, Pearce's friend and fellow Baptist pastor, wrote, "Was much revived and quickened by reading the *Memoirs* of our dear brother Pearce. Felt ashamed that I lived so little like him."[38] Nor was he alone in this feeling. Writing to John Ryland from India, William Carey, whom many regarded as a spiritual giant, said:

> I am delighted with the Life of dear Pearce, but never was I so ashamed of myself. O my dear brother, I really think that I never had in me anything worth calling either love to God or love to man. I appear to myself to have never possessed concern for the heathen, tenderness of conscience, faith, zeal, anything worth calling a Christian grace. I am humbled and astonished.[39]

It may be fitting to close this chapter with a word about the legacy of godliness Pearce left in his family. Sarah Pearce outlived her husband by only five years, but she bore much of his spirit in her own brief life. Writing to a friend, she says that she had learned to dread nothing so much as the guidance of her own blind desires, and to tremble at the thought of such a fatal liberty. She had not the least disposition to think hard thoughts of God. She wished to love and adore him.[40]

Of Pearce's children, little Samuel died shortly after his father, but two others lived to serve God in the place their father had longed to see, the country of India. William Hopkins Pearce (1794–1840) went to Calcutta in 1817, where he founded and made self-supporting the Baptist Mission Press. In time, this press printed Scriptures, tracts and books for Christian schools, while he advocated the cause of female education, and he sought to pastor a local congregation.[41]

Pearce's second daughter, Anna Pearce (1795–1832), also went to India in 1822, encouraged by her brother's desire to see Indian women better educated. She doggedly pursued this good work until her early death.[42] In 1824, she married William Carey's son, Jonathan. Of this marriage their grandson wrote: "It was an abiding satisfaction to Carey that one of his sons, and that the youngest, should be wedded to a daughter of his most revered friend, and that they who had been united in heart should now be united in family."[43]

The lines of Henry Wadsworth Longfellow gather up the legacy of Pearce to all of us who read of him today:

> *Lives of great men all remind us,*
> *We can make our lives sublime,*
> *And, departing, leave behind us*
> *Footprints on the sands of time.*[44]

Of course, apart from God, as Pearce would certainly remind us, we can do nothing. Let this be the legacy of the "seraphic Pearce" to our generation.

ENDNOTES

SECTION I

Chapter 1: What do we mean by "the Word of God"?

1. For discussions of the origin of the phrase see the standard commentaries, especially, George R. Beasley-Murray, *Word Biblical Commentary: John* (Waco: Word, 1987), 6–11, and D.A. Carson, *The Gospel According to John* (Grand Rapids: Eerdmans, 1991), 114–17.

2. We are not even certain how God conveys his will to spirit beings, but it seems likely that the idea contained in the word "speech" is suitable here, much as it was in Genesis 1:3: "Then God said, 'Let there be light'…"

3. See for example John 8:32,45 where Jesus speaks the Word of God and describes it as truth. See also John 17:17, "Sanctify them by the truth; your Word is truth."

4. This statement, of course, begs another set of questions about textual and translation theory that we simply cannot pursue in a short chapter. Most scholars, I think, would agree about most of our committee translations, though some might question the orthodoxy of the producers of a few of them.

5. For the statistically minded, here is the breakdown: (1) Thirty-two meanings simply as a verb; (2) twenty-three in idioms that contain the verb; (3) eighteen meanings as a noun; (4) one meaning in an idiom that contains the noun; (5) sixteen meanings as an adjective, and (6) two meanings in idioms that contain the adjective. (No, I do not guarantee that I counted perfectly!)

6. James Barr, *The Bible in the Modern World* (New York: Harper & Row, 1973) 178. From the same page scholars will enjoy Barr's equally forthright defense of the importance of the Hebrew vowel points. Barr rejects anything like inspiration in any sense that would appeal to conservatives, but he recognizes that if the subject is to be discussed, the discussion must center on the words and letters, including the vowel points.

Chapter 2: The person of Christ as the work of Christ

1. Unfortunately the division of God's attributes into communicable (shareable) and incommunicable (unshareable) is not airtight. For example, infinite wisdom is God's alone. On the other hand, he can and does give men a *small* amount of wisdom.

For discussion of this problem see Wayne Grudem, *Systematic Theology* (Grand Rapids: Zondervan, 1994), 156–157.

2. John 3:34b as it stands alone is ambiguous. It might also mean that "Jesus gives the Spirit [to men] without measure." But the rendering I have put in the text is most consistent with verse 35. The Father, in giving Jesus the Spirit, has also given him ability to do all kinds of things that he could not otherwise do as a man.

3. I pass over here other meanings of "righteousness" applicable to both God and man. Some of these are thought to be closely connected with the covenants of Scripture, but for our purpose we are interested in the character of God logically prior to all covenantal activity. Righteousness in men, of course, arises from God's covenantal work in them.

4. The words in quotation marks are taken from the margin of my Bible, but I no longer know the source, whether myself or someone else.

5. B.B. Warfield, *The Person and Work of Christ* (Philadelphia: Presbyterian and Reformed, 1950), 107. He adds: "We should know...without instruction that Jesus, living in the conditions of this earthly life under the curse of sin, could not fail to be subject to the whole series of angry emotions...[and that] there have been preserved records of the manifestation in word and act of not a few of them."

6. The uncertainty about the number of occurrences reflects the fact that the United Bible Societies' Greek text omits verse 14.

7. The evidence for these assertions is found in the mutual love of Father and Son (see John 14:31; 17:24). Given the equality and likeness among the persons of the Trinity, the participation of the Spirit in these same relations seems a reasonable inference.

Chapter 4: For whom did Christ die?

1. Walter A. Elwell, ed., *Evangelical Dictionary of Theology* (2nd ed.; Grand Rapids: Baker Book House Co./Carlisle, Cumbria: Paternoster Press, 2001), 97–98.

2. I refer to Walter Bauer, *A Greek-English Lexicon of the New Testament*, trans. and adapted William F. Arndt and F. Wilbur Gingrich, and rev. and augmented F. Wilbur Gingrich and Frederick W. Danker (2nd ed.; Chicago/London: University of Chicago Press, 1979), s.v. In what appears to be an effort to reduce the meaning of anti to in behalf of, they have the strange statement, "Genesis 44:33 shows how the meaning in place of can develop into in behalf of...". This, of course, would not require substitution. But anyone who reads Genesis 44:33 will see there as plain a case of substitution as can possibly be imagined. It records the offer of Judah to become a slave in the place of his brother, Benjamin. In the words of the NASV, "Please let your servant remain instead of the lad a slave to my lord, and let the lad go up with his brothers." In other words, he offered to substitute himself for the boy.

3. The Christians who can say no more than this are those who are called "Four-Point Calvinists" and those called "Semi-Pelagians." It is beyond the scope of this study to go into these terms in any detail. Briefly, Four-Point Calvinists believe most of the Calvinistic system including unconditional election and effectual (irresistible) grace, but they deny the particularity of Christ's death. Semi-Pelagians believe that, after the fall, man retained the ability to turn to God. Calvinists deny this.

4. Tom Wells, *A Price for a People, the Meaning of Christ's Death*, Edinburgh: Banner of Truth Trust, 1992.

5. Some members of the early church found in the word *world* a reference to the new humanity that God is forming in Christ. The *Martyrdom of Polycarp* (*c.* AD 150–180) speaks of our Lord as the one who suffered for the whole world of those being saved. Christ has a world of his own, in this understanding, that he is bringing to himself. Origen (*c.* AD 185–254), after citing the words "God was in Christ reconciling the world" (2 Corinthians 5:19) says, "Of the world of the church this is written." He also cites John 1:29 as illustrating the same truth. The sin of the world is for him the sin of the church. For more illustrations of this use from the early church, consult my *A Price for a People: the Meaning of Christ's Death* (Edinburgh: Banner of Truth Trust, 1992), 125–26.

Chapter 5: Misunderstandings of grace

1. This passage may be understood in a slightly different way that gives the same result. The foundation may be taken as the teaching concerning Christ, rather than as Christ himself. In that case the preacher or teacher will be adding further truths to the foundation, or what appear to him to be truths. Then, to the extent that what he has taught is false, to that extent his work will be burned up, though he will be saved. Either understanding is possible. Both preserve the clear intent of Paul here to describe the work of teaching that he and Apollos engaged in, in raising "God's building" (1 Corinthians 3:9). What is plain in either case is that Paul is not endorsing the idea that men may lead ungodly lives and still be saved.

2. I have an unidentified clipping from *Sound of Grace*, edited by John Reisinger, to thank for the way this and the following misunderstanding are worded.

3. But nothing is beyond controversy. History shows that some few theologians have held to what is called "eternal justification," the view that God never held his elect guilty, even before he created them.

SECTION II

Chapter 7: The Epistle to the Hebrews and worship

1. Thomas Watson, *A Body of Divinity* (Repr. London: Banner of Truth, 1958), 5.

2. In speaking of Hebrews as he rather than it, I am taking a cue from Barnabas Lindars [*The Theology of the Letter to the Hebrews* (Cambridge: Cambridge University Press, 1991), xi–xii]. When you meet the word *Hebrews* it will sometimes mean the *author of Hebrews*. In that way I avoid the frequent use of the longer phrase. We do not, of course, know who the author is, so it is impossible to cite him by name.

3. "In His Son" could also be translated "in nothing less than a Son!"

4. The same three contrasts are in Hebrews 2:2–3 where, however, angels replace prophets. By speaking of angels, Hebrews shows that the time past that chiefly interests him is the time of the Mosaic covenant. Angels played a role in its delivery

(compare Deuteronomy 33:2; Psalm 68:17; Acts 7:38,53; Galatians 3:19).

5. Psalm 110 is alluded to or cited extensively in the New Testament—about 20 times. Hebrews refers to it repeatedly. See 1:3,13; 5:6; 6:20; 7:17,21; 8:1; 10:12; 12:2. "Buchanan's definition of Hebrews 'as a homiletical midrash based on Ps. 110…is too constricting, but there is no denying the importance of this psalm throughout the epistle" [Ellingworth, *The Epistle to the Hebrews* (Grand Rapids: Eerdmans, 1993), 129–130].

6. We must not suppose that the Mosaic Law failed to accomplish the purposes for which God gave it. But it did not accomplish the believer's direct access to God. That awaited the work of Christ.

7. The "outer tabernacle" in this verse may mean the same as in verse 6, i.e., the first room in the tabernacle. But here its presence implies the ongoing Mosaic Covenant with its priestly service. As long as that first room remained, the tabernacle and its ministry remained in force.

8. It is the view of the majority of scholars that the Gentiles in view are Gentiles generally, not those who have come to Christ. For the contrary view see C.E.B. Cranfield, *The Epistle to the Romans* (Edinburgh: T. & T. Clark, 1975), I, 155ff.

Chapter 8: The Book of Revelation and the subject of worship

1. See the standard commentaries for discussions of the Holy Spirit in this verse. While the Spirit is merely mentioned here, later passages cite his activity. In chapters 2 and 3 he is repeatedly described as the one who speaks to the churches (Revelation 2:7,11,17,29; 3:1,6,13,22), evidently as the agent of the Lord Jesus. See also Revelation 14:13 and 22:17.

2. James B. Ramsey, *Revelation* (Repr. Edinburgh: Banner of Truth Trust, 1977), 61–62.

3. Who these *angels* are has been the subject of extensive debate. Many have taken them to be pastors or other representatives of the seven congregations since the word "angel" can also mean "messenger." For other options see the discussion in G.R. Beasley-Murray, *The Book of Revelation* (Repr. Grand Rapids: Eerdmans, 1983), 68–70. He leans toward the view that the angels are the " heavenly counterparts of the earthly congregations," a complex idea requiring a good deal of explanation, which he proceeds to give it.

4. See the standard commentaries for discussions of who God's people are in Revelation. Some think they are men of the first century, the *preterist* view. Others think they are believers in the end times, the *futurist* view. George Eldon Ladd in *A Commentary on the Revelation* (Grand Rapids: Eerdmans, 1972), 14, wrote: "[W]e conclude that the correct method of interpreting the Revelation is a blending of the preterist and futurist methods. The beast is both Rome and the eschatological Antichrist—and, we might add, any demonic power which the church must face in her entire history."

5. Leon Morris, *The Book of Revelation* (Grand Rapids: Eerdmans, 1969), 91.

6. In English *worship* and *worthiness* derive from the same root: to worship is to declare someone's worth. Though the Greek words do not have any etymological connection, verses 10 and 11 reflect this intersection of ideas.

7. Richard Bauckham, *God Crucified* (Grand Rapids: Eerdmans, 1999), 62.

8. It is often assumed that the woman in chapter 12 is thought to be the virgin Mary by the Roman Catholic church. A footnote in a modern English Catholic New Testament, however, reads as follows: "12, 1: *A woman*: this woman is not the Blessed Virgin, for the details of the prophecy do not fit her. The prophecy pictures the Church of the Old and New Covenants...By accommodation, the Church applies this verse to the Blessed Virgin." The quotation is from the so-called "Confraternity Edition,"—*The New Testament of Our Lord and Savior Jesus Christ* (Paterson, New Jersey: St. Anthony Guild Press, 1941), 721.

Chapter 9: Unity among Christians and subscription to creeds

1. *Introducing the Free Reformed Churches of North America* (St. Thomas, Ontario: Free Reformed Publications, 1996), 15.

2. The quotation comes from Edward Winslow, *Hypocrisie Unmasked* (London, 1646). It is found in Walter H. Burgess, *John Robinson: Pastor of the Pilgrim Fathers, A Study of His Life and Times* (London: Williams and Norgate, 1920), 239–40.

3. *The Book of Concord* (1580) contains a number of documents going back to the Apostles' Creed that might be described as "articles of faith" by Lutherans, but Flacius wrote this in 1567. He may have intended much more than the *Augsburg Confession*, however. In addition to a number of creeds from the early church, other candidates for articles of faith include the *Apology of the Augsburg Confession* (1531), the *Smalcald Articles* (1537) and the *Treatise on the Power and Primacy of the Pope* (1537), all of which appear in the later *Book of Concord*. It is plain to see that if any of these was also in Flacius' mind, it complicates the problem immensely, especially in the view of someone outside the Lutheran tradition.

4. Both the quotation from Flacius and Fuller's comment are taken from Danile P. Fuller, "Biblical Theology and the Analogy of Faith," in Robert A. Guelich, ed., *Unity and Diversity in New Testament Theology* (Grand Rapids: Eerdmans, 1978), 198.

5. Quoted in Brian G. Armstrong, *Calvin and the Amyraut Heresy* (Madison, Wisconsin: University of Wisconsin, 1969), 134.

6. Norbert Ward, ed., *Beloved Brethren: Circular Letters of the Philadelphia Baptist Association from 1774 to 1807* (Nashville, Tennessee: Baptist Reformation Review, n.d. [c.1970s]). Though Ward was editor, the chapter from which the quotation was taken apparently has no editorial work within it, since it seems plainly to be photocopied from a nineteenth-century page.

7. D.A. Carson, "New Testament Theology," in Ralph P. Martin and Peter H. Davids, eds., *Dictionary of the Later New Testament and Its Developments* (Downers Grove, Illinois: InterVarsity, 1997), 796.

Chapter 10: Baptism and the unity of Christians

1. I have placed "modes" in quotation marks because of the widespread view, often insisted upon by Baptists and supported by others, that the word "baptism" itself describes mode by literally meaning "dipping" or "immersion." In this view the phrase

"mode of baptism" means "mode of immersion" and, hence, is redundant.

2. Immersionists, in addition to holding that "baptism" and "immersion" are synonyms, cite texts like Acts 8:38–39 and Romans 6:4–5. Those who pour cite Acts 1:5 with 2:33 and 10:44–45. Those who sprinkle emphasize texts in which cleansing is prominent (such as Acts 22:16 and Titus 3:5) as well as the situation at Pentecost in which they see the unlikelihood of so many being immersed in a short time.

3. See standard reference works under *Novatians and Donatists.*

4. This, of course, is an oversimplification in the interests of not discussing biblical interpretation in a short chapter. "Figurative sense" is the obvious sense in many contexts and, hence, requires no "burden of proof."

5. Donald Bridge and David Phypers, *The Water that Divides* (Downers Grove, Illinois: InterVarsity, 1977). It was reprinted by Christian Focus Publications in 1998.

6. Douglas Wilson, *To a Thousand Generations* (Moscow, Idaho: Canon Press, 1996), 5. The book shows beyond doubt that Wilson himself is a dedicated paedobaptist, but in his congregation he has sought to accommodate the feelings and convictions of others.

7. For example, P.K. Jewett, *Infant Baptism and the Covenant of Grace* (Grand Rapids: Eerdmans, 1978).

8. H.F Stander and J.P. Louw, *Baptism in the Early Church* (Garsfontein, South Africa: Didaskalia, 1988). At the time of publication, the authors were professors in the University of Pretoria, South Africa.

Chapter 13: Motives for evangelism

1. C.S. Lewis, *Mere Christianity* (New York: Scribner, 1952), 94.

2. Michael Green, *Evangelism in the Early Church* (Grand Rapids: Eerdmans, 1970), 236.

Chapter 14: On the ethics of controversy

1. The article appears in Craig A. Blaising and Darrell L. Bock, eds., *Dispensationalism, Israel and the Church* (Grand Rapids: Zondervan, 1992), 293–328. The two quotations are taken respectively from pages 295 and 294. The italics are Barker's.

2. This is not in the least to deny that real progress has been made over the centuries in the conduct of controversy. We shake our heads over the tone of argument in the writings of many of the men of the past whom we highly value on other grounds.

3. See the interesting illustration of General George Washington and Major André cited by Robert L. Dabney, *Discussions: Evangelical and Theological* (London: Banner of Truth, 1967), I, 285–286.

4. J.C. Ryle, *Knots Untied* (31st ed.; London: Jas. Clarke & Co, 1954).

5. *The Complete Works of the Rev. Andrew Fuller* (London: Henry Bohn, 1859), 317. The italics are in the original.

6. *The Works of Jonathan Edwards* (Edinburgh: Banner of Truth, 1976), I, 529. The italics are in the original.

7. I am unpersuaded by efforts to confine this truth to members within a single

local church, as some have tried to do. It seems clear to me that Paul's words in 1 Corinthians 12:12–13 show that he has the universal church in view.

8. It is clear to me that some parts of the tradition that Pentecostalism represents have, in fact, veered too far from the truth to be considered Christian. (Perhaps they would return the compliment.) But the illustration does not require that every Pentecostal and every Calvinistic Baptist be a true believer. It would be just as true *even if both sides proved to be mainly unbelieving.*

9. D.A. Carson, *The Gagging of God* (Grand Rapids: Zondervan, 1996), 360. This comment is part of a chapter entitled "On Drawing Lines When Drawing Lines Is Rude." The entire chapter is worthy of study. Among other things, see the discussion of the book *Essentials: A Liberal-Evangelical Dialogue* on pages 358–360.

10. *Complete Works of the Rev. Andrew Fuller*, 841.

11. Stephen L. Carter, *The Culture of Disbelief* (New York: Basic Books, 1993), 76.

12. This is taken from an article entitled "Packer the Picketed Pariah," *Christianity Today*, 37, No. 1, 11.

13. *Gagging of God*, 439–440.

14. The words are taken from an unidentified work of J.C. Ryle. I found them in the magazine, *Reformed Theonomy*, 1, No. 2, 4.

SECTION III

Chapter 15: The sources of our sanctification

1. Jonathan F. Bayes, *The Weakness of the Law* (Carlisle, UK: Paternoster Press, 2000). The book is a useful addition to the discussion of the Christian and the law. Despite the suggestion of the title, however, in general it defends the traditional Puritan position.

2. Bayes, *Weakness*, 4.

3. Bayes, *Weakness*, 4.

4. This is too broad a topic to defend in a brief article such as this. There are many good works on the subject of law that have appeared in the past 20 years. Let me suggest some that are not at all widely known. John G. Reisinger, *But I Say Unto You...* (Southbridge, Massachusetts: Crowne, 1989) [available from Sound of Grace, 5317 Wye Creek Dr., Frederick, MD 21703]. Jon Zens has written "This is My Beloved Son, Hear Him!" in a triple issue of the magazine *Searching Together*, 25, Nos. 1, 2, 3 [available from Box 548, St. Croix, WI 54024]. May I also suggest a new book, Tom Wells and Fred Zaspel, *New Covenant Theology*. You may also consult the entire issue of *Reformation & Revival Journal*, 6, No. 3 (Summer 1997), which is devoted to the New Covenant.

5. The prophets in this verse are evidently the New Testament prophets. This is conceded by most modern commentators on the basis of the context. Ephesians 3:5 reads as follows: "In former generations this mystery was not made known to humankind, as it has now been revealed to his holy apostles and prophets by the

Spirit..." The "prophets" here are the New Testament, or Christ's, prophets.

6. It is very important to emphasize that such acts must be understood from instruction based on the Word of God to be effective. This fact has made most Evangelicals very skittish about multiplying symbolic acts beyond those authorized by Scripture. The meanings of baptism and the Lord's table are explained both by Scripture and, generally speaking, by the ministers that perform them. A symbol is a type of picture, but pictures are seldom self-explanatory. Where they are not understood they quickly minister to superstition.

Chapter 16: The holiness of God and the assurance that I am a Christian

1. From Thomas Willcox (1621–1687), *Coming to Christ* (Repr. Pensacola: Chapel Library, abbrev. version).

Chapter 18: What should we pray for?

1. For more of Paul's prayer along this line, see Ephesians 1:17–19a, Philippians 1:9–11; and Colossians 1:9–12.

2. For simplicity's sake I have omitted discussing the words "as we also have forgiven our debtors." They may introduce a condition, but that condition is also part of the request, so the request remains certain of fulfillment.

3. I am frankly uncertain about what the first half of this request means, so I am treating it as a negative way of asking the same thing that we ask in the second half. If the first half is a separate request, it may be an exception to the point I am making about the certainty of these requests. If so, however, it is the only exception in this prayer.

SECTION IV

Chapter 20: Samuel Pearce

1. George Redford and John Angell James, eds., *The Autobiography of the Rev. William Jay* (2nd ed.; London: Hamilton, Adams & Co, 1855), 374.

2. *Commenting and Commentaries* (Repr. Grand Rapids: Kregel, 1954), 4.

3. Andrew Fuller, *Memoirs of the Rev. Samuel Pearce* [*The Complete Works of the Rev. Andrew Fuller*, ed. Joseph Belcher (1845 ed.; repr. Harrisonburg, Virginia: Sprinkle Publications, 1988), III, 369]. Fuller, the leading theologian among Baptists of his day and a man at the forefront of the missionary cause, was Pearce's close friend. Any account of Pearce's life is necessarily heavily dependent on the *Memoirs*.

4. To get an impression of the situation and atmosphere that Pearce entered at Bristol see Michael A.G. Haykin, *One heart and one soul: John Sutcliff of Olney, his friends and his times* (Darlington, Co. Durham: Evangelical Press, 1994), 48–67, where he discusses the Academy as it was about 15 years earlier.

5. Fuller, *Memoirs* (*Works*, III), 370-371.

6. Fuller, *Memoirs* (*Works*, III), 377. Italics are in the original.

7. Fuller, *Memoirs* (*Works*, III), 427-429. Many of these words focus on the goodness, faithfulness and sovereignty of God as we will see shortly

8. Fuller, *Memoirs* (*Works*, III), 372 quotes him as writing, "Our number of members is about 295, between forty and fifty of whom have joined us since I saw you, and most of them I have the happiness of considering as my children in the faith." The letter was written on May 9, 1792, to his close friend from Bristol Academy days, William Steadman. I have used it as the basis of my estimate, on the assumption that it covers his whole period of ministry at Cannon Street up to that time.

9. "The Spirituality of Samuel Pearce," *Reformation Today*, 151 (May/June 1996), 18. As early as February 8, 1793, Pearce wrote to his friend William Steadman, "[O]ur members are between three and four hundred. The word has been remarkably blessed. In less than five months I baptized nearly forty persons, almost all newly awakened" [Fuller, *Memoirs* (*Works*, III), 379].

10. For a description of the meeting see Haykin, *One heart and one soul*, 218–225. The quotation from S. Pearce Carey is from Haykin, *One heart and one soul*, 220.

11. Haykin, *One heart and one soul*, 219.

12. Fuller, *Memoirs* (*Works*, III), 379.

13. Ernest A. Payne, "Some Samuel Pearce Documents," *The Baptist Quarterly*, 18 (1959–1960), 28. The whole document (ibid., 27–29) is worth reading for the amount of light it throws on Pearce as he considers world missions.

14. Fuller, *Memoirs* (*Works*, III, 379–380).

15. J.H. Worman "Samuel Pearce" in John McClintock and James Strong, eds., *Cyclopaedia of Biblical, Theological, and Ecclesiastical Literature* (New York: Harper, 1890), 855.

16. Fuller, *Memoirs* (*Works*, III), 392.

17. Fuller, *Memoirs* (*Works*, III), 396.

18. *The History of Dissenters* (2nd ed., London: Frederick Westley & A.H. Davis, 1833), 652.

19. Fuller, *Memoirs* (*Works*, III), 409. The letter is to a Mr. King, otherwise unidentified by Fuller, but probably one of the Cannon Street deacons, Thomas King. The letter reveals that King had seen what was happening to his pastor and had sent an apothecary to advise Pearce of his danger.

20. Fuller, *Memoirs* (*Works*, III, 368).

21. For a description of High Calvinism and "The Calvinistic Baptists in the eighteenth century," see Haykin, *One heart and one soul*, 15–33 along with the works cited there.

22. The Marrow Controversy was occasioned by the reissuing of a Puritan book entitled *The Marrow of Modern Divinity* early in the eighteenth century. The book was attributed to Edward Fisher of London in 1645 and opposed restricting the offer of salvation in Christ to those who had some previous qualifications to be saved. It should not be confused with William Ames (1576–1633), *The Marrow of Theology*, which was a compendium of systematic Calvinistic theology.

23. For the influence of Edwards on this circle, see Iain H. Murray, *Jonathan Edwards—A New Biography* (Edinburgh: The Banner of Truth Trust, 1987), 456, 470.

24. Jonathan Edwards, *A Divine and Supernatural Light* (1733) [*The Works of Jonathan Edwards* (Repr. Edinburgh: The Banner of Truth Trust, 1974), 2:14].

25. Fuller, *Memoirs* (*Works*, III), 371.

26. S. Pearce Carey, *Samuel Pearce M.A., The Baptist Brainerd* (3rd ed.; London: Carey Press, n.d.), 98. Italics added. S. Pearce Carey was the great-grandson of both Samuel Pearce and William Carey through the marriage of Anna Pearce (Samuel Pearce's daughter) to Jonathan Carey (William Carey's youngest son).

27. Carey, *Samuel Pearce*, 199–200.

28. Carey, *Samuel Pearce*, 201.

29. *Faithful Men; or, Memorials of Bristol Baptist College, and Some of its Most Distinguished Alumni* (London: Alexander & Shepheard, 1884), 155–156.

30. Cited Carey, *Samuel Pearce*, 15.

31. Fuller, *Memoirs* (*Works*, III), 433.

32. Carey, *Samuel Pearce*, 127.

33. Fuller, *Memoirs* (*Works*, III), 422. The nineteenth-century Lutheran theologian, Charles P. Krauth, called Schwartz "the greatest of missionaries of all time" [*The Conservative Reformation and Its Theology* (Philadelphia: United Lutheran Publishing House, 1871), 156].

34. Fuller, *Memoirs* (*Works*, III), 434.

35. Fuller, *Memoirs* (*Works*, III), 436.

36. Fuller, *Memoirs* (*Works*, III), 437.

37. Carey, *Samuel Pearce*e, 217.

38. Carey, *Samuel Pearce*, 220.

39. Carey, *Samuel Pearce*, 220.

40. Carey, *Samuel Pearce*, 221–222.

41. Carey, *Samuel Pearce*, 223.

42. Carey, *Samuel Pearce*, 224–226.

43. Carey, *Samuel Pearce*, 225.

44. H.W. Longfellow, *The Reaper and the Flowers*.

INDEX

love of, 23–24
and praying, 186–189, 195–198
Priest, 77–80
righteousness of, 19–22
Son of God, 14, 74–75
wisdom of, 16–17
wrath of, 22–23
1 John, 177–180

King James Version, 5–6
Kingdom of God, 119–129

Landmark Baptists, 112–113
Law, the, 164, 167–171
Lewis, C.S., 139–140
Limited atonement, see Particular
   redemption
Lord's Prayer, 59–60, 173, 187,
   190–191, 196–198
Luther, Martin, 29, 63–70, 103

Mary, mother of Jesus, 13, 35, 53
Monophysitism, 28–29, 34

Owen, John, 40

Packer, J.I., 157
Particular redemption, 37–49
Pearce, Samuel, 209–223
   admiration of, 209–210
   and Cannon Street Baptist
      Church, 211–212
   children of, 222–223
   doctrine of, 216–219
   early years of, 210–211
   and missions, 212–215
   significance of, 219–223
Pearce, Sarah, 211, 215, 222
Pelagius, Pelagianism, 64–65
Penal substitution, 40–45
Philadelphia Association, 106
Piety, see Sanctification
Prayer, 171–173, 185–192, 193–200
Preaching, 119–129, 131–138

Propitiation, 43–44
Puritans, Puritanism, 167–170

Reformation, 63–70
Revelation, Book of, 87–98
Revival, 201–206
Robinson, John, 101–102
Ryle, J.C., 151

Sanctification, 163–174
   feelings and, 173–174
   goal of, 164–165
   prayer and, 171–173
   sacraments and, 173
   Scripture and, 166–167
   sources of, 163–174
Schaeffer, Francis, 158
Schwartz, C.F., 220
Scripture, 3–11
   verbal inspiration of, 7
   and sanctification, 166–167
   Word of God and, 3–11, 151
Second London Confession (1689), 106
Son(s) of God, 13–14, 74–75
Spurgeon, C.H., 209–210
Steadman, William, 213, 221

Tennent, Gilbert, 203–206
Thomas, John, 213
Total depravity, 63–70
Trinity, 87–88

Unity of Christians, 99–109, 111–118

Warfield, B.B., 48
Westminster Larger Catechism, 192
Will of God, 120–124
Willcox, Thomas, 180
Wilson, Douglas, 115–116
Word of God, see Scripture
Worship, 73–85
   in Hebrews, 73–85
   in Revelation, 87–98

Other titles
available from

www.joshuapress.com

"Godly men wrote this book, putting it in plain, easy-to-understand language... I warmly commend this volume to anyone who wants to grow in his or her understanding of God's Word." — DONALD S. WHITNEY

"I found it wonderfully refreshing...It engages the controversies but is more pastoral than polemical...I commend it to new and seasoned Christians alike." — MARK COPPENGER

a foundation for life

A study of key Christian doctrines and their application

Michael A.G. Haykin, editor

Contributors
David Aspinall, Pierre Constant, Heinz G. Dschankilic, Keith M. Edwards, Jim Elliff, David Kay, Stephen Kring, Jerry Marcellino, David B. Morris, Carl Muller, Peter Pikkert, Don Theobald, Kirk Wellum, Stephen J. Wellum, Fred G. Zaspel

A foundation for life

A study of key Christian doctrines and their application

Edited by Michael A.G. Haykin

Are you trying to understand what the Christian faith is all about? Does studying Christian doctrine seem impractical to your daily life? Do you find some biblical teachings confusing? When things happen in your life do you find yourself questioning God's character? Are you confused about judgment? sanctification? sin? With these and many other questions in our minds, we have brought together some contemporary pastors and church leaders to help explain the basic doctrines of the Christian faith in an easy, understandable way. After all, throughout history, the Bible has provided the surest foundation for living that this world can offer! The impact of this truth should transform your life and help to renew our twenty-first century society. *Ideal for personal or group study.*

ISBN 1-894400-17-8, 144 pages, 6 x 9", perfectbound, softcover

Order online at www.joshuapress.com

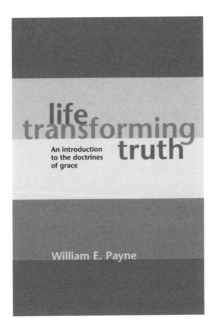

Life-transforming truth

An introduction to the doctrines of grace

by William E. Payne

Have you ever read the Bible and questioned the love of God? Are you perplexed about how God works in individual lives? Why are some people saved and not others? What does it mean to be a child of God? What does it mean to have faith in Christ? What is the real problem of humanity? Some of the truths of God's Word are difficult to understand. Using simple language and a solid biblical foundation, Pastor Payne answers these profound questions as he explains and amplifies the doctrines of grace. He shows how God works in people's lives to show them their need of salvation, how God saves and how God provides eternal hope for those who trust in Christ. He reveals the glory of salvation and its life-transforming effect on the life of the true Christian. *Ideal for personal or group study.*

ISBN 1-894400-11-9, 80 pages, 6 x 9", perfectbound, softcover

Order online at www.joshuapress.com

Heavenly fire

The life and ministry of William Grimshaw of Haworth

by Esther Bennett

Nestled in the rugged hills of West Yorkshire, Haworth was a bleak, working-class village in eighteenth-century England. As the Evangelical Revival was spreading throughout England and America, William Grimshaw was preaching the gospel and leading many in this northern town and its vicinity to faith in Christ. His unflagging labours extended to the surrounding towns for miles around, and when men like George Whitefield and John Wesley, key figures and leading preachers of their day, visited Haworth on their preaching tours, they were witness to the tremendous awakening and spiritual vitality that had been wrought in men and women through the ministry of Grimshaw. This brief sketch of Grimshaw's life will bring you face-to-face with a humble man whose "heavenly fire" was used to transform poor villagers into those who knew the riches of Christ. This is a great introduction to Grimshaw!

ISBN 1-894400-08-9, 24 pages, 8 x 8", saddle-stitch, colour, softcover

Order online at www.joshuapress.com

Fierce the conflict

by Norman H. Cliff

Much is known about the miraculous survival and rapid growth of the church in China in the half century following Liberation, but relatively little is known about the courageous stand that many individual Christians took in the difficult days of the "Accusation Meetings" and the traumatic ten years of the Cultural Revolution.

Fierce the conflict relates the hardship and struggle of eight believers whose faith was tested through periods of persecution, imprisonment and forced labour. These carefully documented stories illustrate the sustaining grace of God and will challenge readers to examine their own fidelity to Christ. The author, Dr. Norman Cliff, was born in China to missionary parents and his first-hand knowledge of the country and some of the believers profiled in this volume makes the telling of these stories that much more personal. This book will open your eyes and heart to the work of God in the vast country of China.

ISBN 1-894400-12-7, 208 pages, 6 x 9", perfectbound, softcover

Order online at www.joshuapress.com

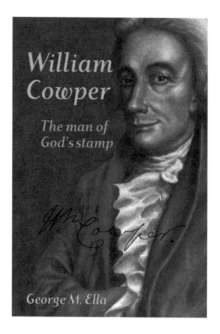

William Cowper
The man of God's stamp
by George M. Ella

William Cowper was an eighteenth-century evangelical poet and translator, renowned for his celebrated gifts and genius. Although highly acclaimed for his poetry in literary and religious circles, the difficult life and deep faith of Cowper have frequently been misunderstood and misinterpreted. In this volume, Dr. George Ella takes a fresh look at the poet and shows how God's stamp thoroughly penetrated Cowper's verse. From the themes, inspiration and theology of his poetry, Dr. Ella shows how that stamp extended throughout Cowper's entire life and even his periods of depression.

This book will make you want to read more of Cowper's poetry and learn more of his God!

ISBN 1-894400-09-7, 240 pages, 6 x 9", perfectbound, softcover

Order online at www.joshuapress.com

Led by the Spirit
How the Holy Spirit guides the believer
by Jim Elliff

What does it mean to follow God? In a personal and pastoral way, Jim Elliff seeks to help the believer gain confidence in understanding and following the will of God. This book is not only practical, but answers some of the most important questions which confuse sincere believers in their desire to do God's will. Jim Elliff emphasizes that guidance has far more to do with sanctified reason than such extraordinary measures as seeing signs or hearing voices. This is a balanced and biblical approach to a vital subject.

ISBN 1-894400-00-3, 48 pages, 4-1/4 x 7", sewn, softcover

Order online at www.joshuapress.com

Deo Optimo et Maximo Gloria
To God, best and greatest, be glory

Cover and book design by Janice Van Eck
Set in Janson Text and Trade Gothic Condensed
Printed in Canada